THE PERPETUAL PAYCHECK

5 Secrets to Getting a Job, Keeping a Job,
and Earning Income for Life
in the Loyalty-Free Workplace

LORI B. RASSAS

DEDICATION

To my parents,
MARGE AND AARON,

and

in memory of my grandparents,
DEBORA AND ISAK
and
MOLLY AND BEN,

who all said I could.

And, a special shout-out to my nieces and nephew,
DANICA, JAMIE, LOGAN, and DAVIS,
who love reading my books, big words and all.

AUTHOR'S NOTE

I have been fortunate enough to have worked in a number of incredibly hospitable environments, where many people took me under their wings and supported my ultimate goals. I would not hesitate to work for any of my prior employers again. Not only that, but most of my prior bosses are aware of this book, have been supportive of this book, and have read drafts of it along the way. So when I use the term "loyalty-free," it is not a reflection of my personal experience with any of my previous employers. Rather, and as I state in my Introduction, the term "loyalty-free" is meant to reflect the short-term and limited-term commitments that, because of ever-changing needs and other mitigating circumstances, widely prevail among employers and employees in today's workplace.

TABLE OF CONTENTS

EMBRACE THE LOYALTY-FREE WORKPLACE

Today should be the best day of your working life. The shriek of your alarm should be music to your ears, because it signals the start of a glorious day. Pour yourself a cup of hot coffee and skip over to your breakfast table with a smile on your face. Today is a great day, because there has never been a better time to be an employee or a job hunter.

I know it might not seem like it right now, but there are more workplace opportunities out there than you could ever imagine. There is simply no reason you should ever again be underpaid or experience an unwanted gap in your employment. This is the perfect environment to ensure that you have a stream of income for life.

First, I'm going to take a stab at why you picked up this book. Perhaps you've responded to ads for about fifty job openings, reached out to ten people for informational interviews, and scheduled a handful of meetings or job interviews. Despite all your efforts, you've yet to receive a job offer. Or, maybe you've excelled in the same job for five years, but continue to be passed over for promotional opportunities. Or you might be changing jobs in the middle of your career, or are out of work for a reason that is no fault of your own.

"It's not exactly the sort of morale booster I had in mind."

Whichever scenario fits you best, I'm fairly certain you have a very strong work ethic. But I'll also bet that you're having trouble fully committing to a robust job search, because it seems like forever since your efforts produced any meaningful results.

How did I do? Well, I understand where you're coming from because I've been exactly where you are. I've experienced the highest workplace highs and some pretty low lows. I've worked at jobs where I was under-appreciated and jobs where I was underpaid. I've applied for jobs, and I've been rejected from jobs. I've met with friends, friends of friends, friends of friends of friends, and even neighbors of friends of friends. I've even met with strangers who were wondering what I was doing and why was I there.

I've been rejected via mail, phone, email, postcard, and text. I've been told no to my face, and I've been told no behind my back. I've been told no in a gentle, kind, and supportive tone, and I've been told no in such a harsh manner I can still feel the sting. In many, many, many cases, I have been completely ignored. I've moved through the interview process with prominent employers that, objectively speaking, should never have considered my application. And, I've been rejected for positions that were a perfect fit.

Once, I made it to the third and final round of interviews for a job to provide legal counsel to the president of a large academic institution. I spent a delightful morning getting to know the university president and was escorted to a catered lunch attended by the entire presidential cabinet. I left that interview confident that a job offer was forthcoming and glad I decided to spend my last paid vacation day from my current job at the event. That was five years ago, and I still haven't heard from them. The only notification I received that I didn't get the job was an announcement on the university's website welcoming the new hire to the presidential team. And this was from a potential employer who consistently marveled at how much value my experience could bring to the institution and who pressured me to rearrange my work schedule to move quickly through their process.

My having gone through what you're going through isn't the only reason you should give my optimism a chance. This is my business. I am a successful employment attorney, career coach, and negotiator. I provide guidance to executives, entertainment personalities, and even recent college graduates. I've worked with people looking for their first internships or entry-level jobs, people looking for career advancement opportunities, and people looking for jobs to take them in entirely new directions. Plus, I've sat on the other side of the desk and have represented employers. I understand how the workplace works from both sides of the fence.

I've also worked as an advocate for employees looking for and trying to keep their jobs, and for employers looking to hire new employees and looking to maintain those currently employed. I've worked in human resources, counseling entry-level employees about the importance of "requesting" a day off instead of "demanding" it. I've counseled employees about how to manage the anxiety associated with reporting to a new supervisor younger than their children. I've worked to develop the skills of employees who had contributed decades of their lives to an employer, only to learn that their inability to create Excel spreadsheets with pivot tables suddenly made them obsolete. I've worked with individuals who were making a lot of money, not making enough money, or making no money at all.

During the course of my work, I have heard hundreds of stories about how people feel about their workplace experiences. When I think about the advice I've provided and the conversations I've had on a consistent basis with every one of these individuals, no matter their situation, there's always one consistent theme: *If you had to pick the most perfect time to be in the job market, it would be now.*

Why? Because there's a general consensus in the workplace that there are only short-term commitments, limited to perhaps 24-hour periods. If an employee performs a full day's work on Monday, the employer is obligated to pay the employee for that time. As for Tuesday, nothing is guaranteed. The employer can tell the employee that his services are no longer needed, just as the employee can inform the employer that he intends to resign. This absence of a mutual obligation creates unprecedented opportunities for advancement and growth.

> "To succeed, it is necessary to accept the world as it is and rise above it."
>
> **MICHAEL KORDA**
> AMERICAN PUBLISHING EXECUTIVE AND AUTHOR

If this seems counterintuitive to you, that's because it most certainly is. Few people recognize what is happening in the workplace. Even *fewer* people are armed with the tools necessary to access those rewards. The good news is that I know the secrets to navigating this new world, and after reading this book, you'll know them as well.

IT IS WHAT IT IS

First things first. It is time to open your eyes to see the world not as you want it to be or think it should be, but as it currently exists. I know things used to be different. Companies were fully staffed, expense accounts were flush, holiday parties were lavish, annual wages were guaranteed, and rapid advancement was inevitable (even if it wasn't deserved). Perhaps some employees did not make significant contributions to the company, but because coworkers were viewed as extended family members, less than stellar employees were tolerated. But, economic realities have set in. General Motors and Lehman Brothers illustrate that this sense of blind loyalty can no longer be supported. The workplace has to focus on what matters: making money.

> **"I yam what I yam."**
>
> **POPEYE**

This situation isn't so unusual. You probably enter into many relationships in which the parties only commit to one another for as long as they need each other.

When you want to rent a new apartment, you develop a list of what you are looking for. You do some research to determine what options are available, you review the pros and cons of different residences, you reach an agreement about the terms, and you sign a lease. During the term of the lease, you and your landlord have certain obligations. You will be required to pay your rent on time, refrain from damaging the apartment, and obey any established rules related to noise and pets. In exchange, your landlord is obligated to provide heat and hot water, to refrain from entering your home unannounced, and to fix any damages within a reasonable amount of time. When the terms of the lease expire, either party is free to move on from the relationship. If a landlord decides to sell the apartment or to rent the apartment to another tenant, both are perfectly acceptable. Similarly, if the tenant decides to move to another apartment, or to purchase a home on their own, they are free to make that decision and no one would hold it against them.

You rent your job. You do not own it. An employee and employer agree that they want to enter into a working relationship. The employee provides a service, and in exchange, the employer offers compensation. In most situations, both the employer and the employee have the right to end the relationship at any time.

> **YOU DON'T OWN YOUR JOB. YOU JUST RENT IT.**

Each day is a recurring obligation: Employee works. Employer pays. Neither party has any obligation beyond that. When the agreed on length of service comes to an end, the relationship ends and neither party owes anything else to the other.

Despite this, most employees have come to expect some sense of loyalty from their employers. Employees believe they have a right to continued employment, a right to a significant annual wage increase, and a right to a promotion after working in a position for an extended period of time. If employers were truly committed to their employees, this might be the result. But most employers today usually aren't committed to their employees. Instead, they're loyal to their shareholders, their boards of directors, and their bank accounts. When the needs of a company change, their needs for employees change.

JUST ONE MORE TEMPORARY RELATIONSHIP

This fluidity isn't all that different from most of our other relationships. Think about your circle of friends. When you're invited to a large social gathering (and are allowed to bring a guest), you immediately contact your outgoing friend who always has his dancing shoes half laced. When you receive two passes to an exclusive book reading and panel discussion, you contact your intellectual friend who's likely to have read the books and be interested in hearing some divergent perspectives. Feeling depressed? You know exactly which friend will support your decision to stay in bed with a pint of ice cream, and which one will scold you for throwing a pity party. We have different relationships for different purposes, and we gravitate to those people who can satisfy a particular need.

Now suppose you get a haircut and hate your look. Where do you find yourself twelve weeks later? Most likely you will be catching up on the community gossip while sitting in another haircutter's styling chair. If your plumber has to return three times to fix the same leak, the next time you need someone to snake a drain, you'll likely hire someone else. You may purchase your first home from one realtor, but your second home from another.

We're not always loyal to contractors or companies when we make decisions as consumers. But when it comes to our career and livelihood, we have a double standard. We often stay at a job well past its shelf life because *we like the people* or *the commute is so convenient* or simply, *it's what we know.*

The purpose of work is to earn a living. Therefore, we should always look for work relationships where we can make the most money. It really is that simple.

IT'S ALL ABOUT THE MONEY

Since it should be all about the money, whether or not you love your job should have nothing to do with your decision to find a new one. Yet you'd be amazed at how many people stay in jobs that don't provide the level of income they need to survive, or remain in jobs despite knowing it's just a matter of time before their source of income will come to an end. Some justify an inadequate income by focusing on their level of comfort with their day-to-day tasks, their love of their boss, the potential for future promotions (which never materialize), or even for the size and location of their office.

We want to believe that we should work in a field that we love. Many of us consider our careers an extension of ourselves. Lots of us are reluctant, embarrassed, or even ashamed to admit that we work for any other purpose. OK, perhaps you have a friend or two who really does get a

> **"**I learned long ago that there's nothing intrinsically wrong with being out of work. It's being out of money that's the problem.**"**
>
> **MARK RENZLER**
>
> A CHARACTER IN THE NOVEL "WHO SHOT LONGSHOT SAM?" BY PAUL ENGLEMAN

bit depressed at the close of business on Friday and cannot wait to come back on Monday morning. Then there are the 99.999999 percent of us who get up and go to work because we need the money to survive. If we are honest with ourselves, we know the primary goal of work is to make money, and so it logically follows that we need to conduct ourselves in a manner that is consistent with this goal.

What's the first thing a lottery winner says when accepting the winning check? "I'm quitting my job!" It's rare to find lottery winners who continue to work, just because they love their jobs. Most leave their current job to do what they have always wanted to do.

There is an ongoing national debate related to whether governments should pass laws requiring employers to provide all employees with some number of paid sick days. This is because many employees, particularly those in lower-paid positions, often report to work sick because staying home would result in a reduced paycheck, which they cannot afford. If they weren't working for the money, they would be home resting.

> "I do my job in a very professional manner. I take money for it every chance I get."
>
> MELANIE WHITE

Have you ever asked for additional time off after exhausting your paid vacation time? Most of us would enjoy one more summer Friday off to spend time at the beach, or perhaps an extra day around the holidays to savor the season. But once our paid leave is depleted, we don't ask for additional time off. Why? Because we work for the money, not the emotional or psychological satisfaction. If your boss said you were entitled to three weeks of paid leave each year, as well as two additional weeks of unpaid leave to use at your discretion, would you use those additional two weeks? Probably not, because we work for the money. When faced with additional work, additional hours, and additional levels of stress, would you ask for additional compensation or say, "thanks for giving me more work, because I love it!"?

While working in a job you do not love might require a philosophical shift for some, it is a shift made necessary by the new workplace environment. In today's workplace, you probably won't be working in any job for more than a few years, so any love you have for your job will not last forever. This is in contrast to the past, where we remained in our jobs for long periods of time. Today, even if you happen to like your job, it's more like dating than marriage. You're looking for a job "with benefits," not a job for life.

Also, in the loyalty-free workplace, just as our jobs are changing, so, too, are the jobs of those around us. This is important to remember because even if we find ourselves in a job we love because of our boss, that, too, is likely to be short-lived. Because of this uncertainty, we have to focus on what we can control—our income—and then use that money to fund what we love and feel passionate about.

In other words, it's not about working in a job we hate. It's about working a job that pays us money so we can fund the things we love.

TAKING RISKS TO BRING HOME A PAYCHECK

I've seen very smart, passionate, and successful people make misguided and, in some cases, potentially dangerous decisions when their income is at risk.

Once, at a negotiation session, I was blindsided by the amount of time we spent talking about the safety of traffic reporters who sometimes delivered their reports in company helicopters as they flew over certain congested areas. The managers were incredibly offended by even the suggestion that they would place their reporters at risk. They insisted that their pilots had full and total discretion to refrain from taking off in weather conditions they deemed dangerous. The problem, we learned, was that pilots were paid based solely on the number of completed flights. If they declined to take off due to weather conditions, they would not get paid. Traffic reporters told us that pilots admitted that when their mortgage or car payment was overdue, they would fly in conditions they might otherwise avoid.

I was once called in to represent Sadie Rangler, 27, a television weather person whose job, I was told, was at risk. I was brought into the situation at the last minute and didn't have time to prepare for the conference call—but as soon as I heard Sadie's scratchy voice, I figured her employer was upset at how many sick days she'd taken. I was wrong. They were upset because she *hadn't* taken sick days.

Classified as a freelance employee, Sadie got paid only when she worked. A tough winter resulted in chronic laryngitis. The station manager told Sadie that she wasn't permitted to report to work until her voice was restored. Sadie explained to me that she barely made enough money to make ends meet, and so she could not miss any more work hours because she needed the money.

Sadie was an individual with a genuine passion for the weather. She always laughed when her colleagues joked that she was so focused on her career, she "had her head in the clouds." If I had a conversation with Sadie at this very moment, she would probably tell me she was not working for money, but that she loved her job and would do it for free. In some other context, I might have believed that, but at the moment it was clear to me that when it came down to it, she was willing to risk it all to get paid.

The point is, even when we say how much we love our jobs, we're really working for the money.

THE DANGER OF FORGETTING THAT IT'S ALL ABOUT THE MONEY

I can speak to this myself. A few years after I graduated law school, I left my first full-time job (with benefits) to enroll in a graduate program and become a student (again), just so I could qualify for an unpaid internship at a large entertainment company. I lived in my childhood bedroom as I went back to school and worked for free, all the time grinning ear to ear because I was fulfilling my dream of working in the entertainment industry.

After completing my program and working at my internship for about thirteen months, I landed an interview for a full-time job in the entertainment industry. I approached the interview with confidence because a number of the people I worked with at my internship knew the interviewer and had provided ringing endorsements of my qualifications. The interviewer and I had a comfortable and spirited conversation. I was fairly certain the job was mine to lose. As the end of our discussion neared, the interviewer slowly closed the file folder on his desk and asked, "Is there anything else you want to add?"

> **"**Desperation works in a job search as well as it does in dating.**"**
>
> **DARRELL GURNEY**
>
> AUTHOR, "NEVER APPLY FOR A JOB AGAIN!: BREAK THE RULES, CUT THE LINE, BEAT THE REST"

Where was my office? What font options are available for my nameplate? Can I get my business card printed vertically instead of horizontally just like the other creative types I had met? These were the questions that were swirling in my mind. But, because I felt like this was my last chance to show how much I wanted this job, I said something like this:

> I just wanted to tell you how grateful I am that you are considering me for this position. I'm sure you have a lot of qualified candidates, but I can assure you that no one wants this job more than me. I spent the last thirteen months basically working for free at an entertainment company to get my foot in the door, and now that I am here, I want you to know I will do anything to make it work. I type more than 90 words a minute, and I will even follow you around in your negotiations, take notes, and type them up for your review. Whatever you need, whatever it takes, I will get it done.

The interviewer smiled at me awkwardly and said:

> I appreciate your enthusiasm, but I can assure you what I don't need is an overpriced note-taker. As we've discussed over the last ninety minutes, I need someone who can get on a plane on a moment's notice en route to a city where others might not necessarily want to travel. Upon arrival, I need someone to negotiate a deal, come back to the office, and get ready for the next assignment. That's what I need. Thanks so much for your time.

Ouch. I showed that I was desperate and love sick for the job, not a qualified savvy professional.

Thankfully, I was offered the job a few hours later. But the comments the interviewer made left a lasting impression on me, and reminded me of the reason that we work. Employers have limited budgets. They need someone to get the work done. They don't care if you think that working for their company would be a dream come true, or that you're willing to do tasks other than those for which they have a need.

I was lucky. Had I made those comments today, I doubt a job offer would have followed. In the loyalty-free workplace, the last emotion you want to broadcast is one of desperation. Here's what I should have said:

> Thank you so much for asking. I am confident that I have the exact skills to hit the ground running. You have a backlog of contracts that need to be negotiated. I'll negotiate them. You have a list of destinations others do not have the time to visit. I am ready to book my flights. I have no concerns about my ability to perform the work, so my only remaining question is whether you have any concerns about my qualifications that I can address.

Professional. No drama. No desperation. He had a need for work to be done, and for the right price I could do it. The only logical next step would have been to make me an offer I could not refuse and put me to work.

YOU MAKE YOUR OWN SANDWICH

There is a classic *Peanuts* comic strip that shows Charlie Brown opening his lunch on a few consecutive days and dreading what he finds. Finally, Lucy asks Charlie Brown who makes his sandwiches. He says that he does! Many of us continue to do the same thing day in and day out, even though it makes us miserable and simply isn't working.

How are your sandwiches? If you've read this far, the answer is probably not so great. Isn't it time to make a new one? Don't you deserve a good job with benefits that provides you with the economic security to live a full life? The answer should be a resounding *yes*, and there has never been a better time to achieve that than now.

This book is not about picking sides or convincing you that employers are bad and employees are good. It's about providing you with a guide to the modern workplace—the loyalty-free workplace—so you can make informed decisions to achieve the most success under the existing circumstances. There's no need to hide this book so that no one sees you reading it. The loyalty-free environment is to be embraced, not denied. There is nothing to fear.

Today really *is* a great day, because improved material benefits are within everyone's reach. The even better news is that by adopting five new attitudes and approaches to navigating this new world, you'll be that much closer to having them in your grasp.

SECRET # 1

CASH IS KING

Many of us grew up thinking that the world would bend to our needs and desires. We were raised with the expectation that work equaled self-actualization, meaning our jobs should provide us psychological, emotional, and material satisfaction in addition to a steady paycheck.

Not to burst anyone's bubble, but in the loyalty-free workplace there isn't time for that. You don't have the luxury of limiting your job search to jobs for which you have passion. But, the good news is that you're not doomed to years in a soul-killing job. Because of the transient nature of today's workplace it's highly unlikely that you'll be in it for the rest of your working life. Instead, the day you start your current job is also when you start looking for the next one.

I'm not suggesting passion isn't important—just the opposite. I *want* you to pursue your passion. I think this is so critical that I want you to control the situation without delegating the achievement of your passion to someone else (particularly an employer whose interests aren't aligned with yours). In the loyalty-free workplace, the only person who cares about your passions is you.

Jared Nickeloff, 62, has worked at the same company for twenty-four years. He's never missed a day of work, nor has he ever reported late to his 9:00am shift. Coworkers are therefore concerned when Jared is not at his designated seat for the regularly scheduled Tuesday morning 9:30 staff meeting.

Six minutes after the meeting starts, Jared stumbles into the meeting room, visibly shaken. "I passed out on the stairs heading down the subway and nearly died," he explains.

His boss replies, "You mean to tell me it took you thirty-six minutes to roll down a flight of stairs?"

OK, this may seem like an extreme example. But the reality is that the boss' comments are perfectly aligned with today's loyalty-free workplace.

If you're Jared's spouse (or perhaps one of his coworkers witnessing this scenario), your natural reaction is to worry about Jared's well-being. If you're Jared's boss, however, your loyalty is to the company first. If Jared cannot function at his job, for the good of the company he'll have to be replaced, notwithstanding his perfect attendance record.

Let's face it: Work is work. No one wakes up in the morning and says, "Have a great day, honey. I'm off to have fun!" More likely you wake up and say, "I really have to get going, or else I'll be late for work." It's a professional obligation, and we have to be professional at all times. That includes always remembering that your role is to contribute to the company's success (which, in turn, will result in continued compensation).

A woman is arguing with her husband over whether he is being aggressive enough about asking for a raise. "You need to tell your boss that you have five children, a sick father, three dogs, and a wife that has to stay up all night cleaning your home because you cannot afford a housekeeper," she insists.

The next day, the husband returns home and announces that he has been fired.

"Why?" yells the wife. "What did you do?"

The husband says, "My boss told me I have too many outside activities."

—UNKNOWN

If you're looking for a job, potential employers could not care less if you're unemployed with a mortgage to pay, growing medical bills, and absolutely, positively need this job. A prospective employer will see this desperation as a distraction that may, and probably will, prevent you from being productive. All a prospective employer wants to know is (a) Do you have the skills that they're looking for and (b) If they hire you, can you hit the ground running and get the job done?

Even if you consider a particular vacancy to be your "dream job," the last thing a hiring manager wants to hear is how excited you are about working for the company. Believe it or not, sharing that information can actually hurt your chances of landing the job. You have to remember that it's not about you—it's about what you can do for the company. In the loyalty-free workplace, making it about you will be a hindrance to your success.

DON'T HIJACK YOUR CHANCES OF LANDING THE JOB

We all know people who hijack conversations. They're the ones who, when we tell them how depressed we are or that we're going through a really bad time, turn it around so that they're talking about *their* problems, instead of listening to ours. In other words, they make themselves the center of attention.

In most cases, you can right the situation by reminding your friend, "Hey, this isn't about you!" But if you hijack a job interview by bringing up something that has nothing to do with the company's needs, you may end up eliminating yourself from further consideration.

At the end of a job interview, a potential employer asks an applicant, "What hourly rate are you looking for?"

"At least $100 per hour," says the applicant.

The interviewer raises her eyes. "That's awfully high for someone with such limited experience."

"My rate takes into account that it is going to be difficult for me to perform tasks that I have never done before," replies the applicant. "Therefore I will require more time to do them."

—UNKNOWN

Employers want what employers want—and almost always get it. The most successful employees today are those who meet their employer's needs in a way that provides the employer with the most significant benefits.

A company is looking for ways to cut costs. In an effort to include its 1,000-employee workforce in the decision-making process, the company offers a $10,000 reward to any employee who comes up with an idea that results in long-term cost reduction. Stan from Accounting proposes that the company slash future annual employee bonuses by 50 percent (from $1,000 to $500), which would save the company $500,000/year. Stan wins the $10,000 prize.

—UNKNOWN

THE CINDERELLA FIT

Back in the days when employers had plenty of staff, they could afford to hire a candidate who was a close fit (as far as qualifications go), but not a perfect one. In some cases, they might even hire people who were clearly *not* qualified for the position, but had enough potential that they

"People say, 'Oh, you were better heavy,' or 'I like you better thick,' and I say, 'It's not about you.'"

JENNIFER HUDSON
ACADEMY AWARD WINNER / ACTRESS
ON HER SLIMMED-DOWN FIGURE

would "find a spot for them." In the loyalty-free workplace, however, that luxury no longer exists. "Pretty good" or "close enough" will not cut it anymore. With more people than ever competing for fewer jobs, companies have to be more selective. Like Prince Charming, prospective employers are looking for the one person who is the perfect fit for that glass slipper—and if it doesn't fit (or if you say something during the interview that suggests you'd be a bad fit), they almost always have a stack of other qualified candidates to consider instead of you.

Walking down the street, a dog sees a sign in an office window:

> HELP WANTED
> MUST TYPE 70 WORDS A MINUTE
> MUST BE COMPUTER LITERATE
> MUST BE BILINGUAL
> EQUAL OPPORTUNITY EMPLOYER

The dog applies for the position, but is quickly refused.

"I can't hire a dog," says the office manager.

The dog points to the line "equal opportunity employer."

The office manager sighs and asks if the dog can type. The dog walks over to a typewriter and flawlessly bangs out a letter.

"Can you operate a computer?" asks the manager. The dog sits down at a terminal, writes a program and runs it perfectly.

"Look, you have fine skills, but I still can't hire a dog," says the exasperated office manager. "I need someone who's bilingual. It says so right in the ad."

The dog looks up at the manager and says, "Meow."

—DONALD WEINSTEIN

In the loyalty-free workplace, you can't be a dog who *might* learn new tricks. If you're granted an interview, you must show the prospective employer right then and there that you know all of the "tricks" necessary to excel at the job. How do you show a prospective employer that you are the perfect fit? By identifying precisely what the employer is looking for and providing it.

TOP THREE MISTAKES THAT JOB SEEKERS MAKE TODAY

If you want to land a job in today's workplace, avoid doing the following:

IGNORING INSTRUCTIONS WHEN SUBMITTING YOUR QUALIFICATIONS

This is probably the most common mistake of all. Time and again, hiring managers tell me about applicants who should have been shoe-in candidates, but were never even considered simply because they did not follow instructions.

Remember, prospective employers don't owe you anything. If they receive a hundred resumes, and fifty of the applicants don't bother with following directions, guess which ones they're going to eliminate? So when applying for any position, provide *everything* that is requested. If the job posting requests a cover letter, be sure to write one. If an employer asks for a writing sample and a list of three references along with an application, provide both. If the directions say to send your application to a particular email address, don't fax it, send it by overnight mail, or drop it off personally—email it. If a prospective employer wanted to consider alternative methods of delivery, the directions would have said so.

Similarly, if a prospective employer says it's OK to contact him or her in a method other than what's stated, follow those instructions—but be sure to comply with any original directions, too. There's a reason for this. As the hiring process moves forward, your application will likely be reviewed by a number of different people, many of whom may not be in constant touch with each other. Just because Sally tells you to send your resume directly to her, that doesn't mean that the human resources director who reviews your resume two weeks later will know why you bypassed the online system.

The same goes for a job listing that says to send applications to a general mailbox. Even if someone in your network tells you to reach out to their hiring manager friend directly, cover your bases and do both. Otherwise, if you try to shortcut the process, you'll end up derailing yourself.

Alberto Reynolds, 31, Rosana Klaver, 34, and Clara Daners, 34, attend a networking event sponsored by their local Italian-American professional organization. All three graduated from the same college as one of the panelists. When the panelist mentions that his friend Carl Rogers, 44, is looking to fill a number of positions at his start-up company, all three locate Carl's company on the Internet and apply for a position. The online posting directs all applicants to email their applications to the general mailbox (with the title of the position in the subject line) and makes it clear that any applications that are sent to individual email addresses will be deleted unread.

Alberto sends his submission only to the general email referenced in the posting, with the title of the position in the subject line. A few weeks later, he receives a generic email reply indicating that the company received applications from a number of qualified candidates and that the position had been filled.

Rosana sends her application directly to Carl, with the title of the position in the subject line. But she never receives a response.

Clara sends her application both directly to Carl and the general email address, along with a cover letter saying that she learned about the position from the presentation at the Italian-American networking event given by Carl's friend. Though Carl had automatically deleted Clara's email application (per the company policy that all applicants go through the general mailbox), the administrative assistant who went through the general mailbox forwarded her email to him after seeing that Clara had mentioned the Italian-American networking event in her cover letter. Clara was the only candidate among the three to receive an interview.

Why did Alberto and Rosana fail, while Clara succeeded? Because their materials never got past the initial entry point for consideration. Unfortunate? Yes, but it happens all the time in a loyalty-free workplace, where companies are understaffed and employees are overworked.

In all likelihood, Carl had a heavy workload, so when he received emails that should have been directed to the general inbox as instructed, he was more than happy to delete them. Once he realized that one of these applicants had been indirectly referred to him by a friend, Carl was willing to take the time to review Clara's resume.

EMPHASIZING THE SKILLS YOU HAVE, BUT IGNORING OR MINIMIZING THE SKILLS YOU DON'T

If a company is looking for a website designer who is skilled in iWeb and Dreamweaver, that means they want a candidate with experience in both programs. No matter how much you talk about your mastery of iWeb, you won't get past the initial review unless you can demonstrate proficiency in both.

Too many candidates believe that if they convince a prospective employer how strong they are in one aspect of the job, their weaknesses with regard to other requirements won't matter. In the loyalty-free workplace, that is a huge mistake. You should only target jobs that line up with your strengths.

Lillian Allen, 29, is having difficulty advancing in her current position in the student development office of a large liberal arts university. An overachiever, she is also incredibly shy. To overcome her shyness, Lillian enrolls in a number of public speaking classes, while also volunteering to make presentations at monthly staff meetings.

Despite her efforts, Lillian is unable to secure a position that requires her to have constant interaction. Given her shyness, it becomes clear to me (even after a short discussion) that Lillian will have a hard time succeeding in a position that requires her to interact with others on a regular basis. However, because Lillian is a very talented writer, we develop a plan that enables her to transition into a grant-writing position at the school. There, she can focus her efforts on improving her already well-developed writing skills (which benefits both her and her employer).

FOCUSING ON WHAT YOU THINK IS IMPORTANT, REGARDLESS OF WHETHER IT HAS ANYTHING TO DO WITH THE TASK AT HAND

The lowest grade I received in high school was in biology. I adored my teacher, enjoyed the class tremendously, and learned a lot. I was in prime position to earn an A—and probably would have, had I not made a strategic mistake on the final exam.

We were given five essay questions in advance. The instructions were to answer any three of them for the final. Because I wanted my teacher to know how much I learned in his class, I decided that the more questions I answered (and, therefore, the more I showed him how much I knew about biology), the better my score would be.

> **"If you don't want to work, you have to work to earn enough money so that you don't have to work."**
>
> **OGDEN NASH**
> ESSAYIST, 1902-1971

Boy, was I wrong. As this was a timed test, and since I chose to answer all five questions, it won't surprise you to learn that my grade was not as high as I had anticipated. Instead of reading all five of my responses, my teacher only read and graded the first three questions. This means that I not only accumulated zero points for my answers to the two ungraded questions, but I hurt myself on the three questions that *were* graded, because I didn't spend as much time answering them as I should have. As a result, I got a lousy score on the final, which hurt my overall grade.

How does this translate to applying for a job in the loyalty-free workplace? By serving as a reminder that employers today want the perfect fit... nothing more, and nothing less. So if you're asked to provide a five-page writing sample, don't send ten pages to show how much you know—stick to five. If a client wants a memo, don't submit a memo along with an accompanying PowerPoint presentation. Not only are you complicating a simple task, you're likely to annoy the employer (and hurt yourself in the process) by showing that you cannot follow instructions.

Once upon a time, an otherwise highly skilled applicant could compensate for any weaknesses simply by saying that she "learns fast and can get up to speed quickly." That doesn't work anymore. Most employers today won't take the time or resources to train you for a position for which you are not fully qualified. They'd just as soon move on to the next applicant until they find their Cinderella fit.

MUCH LESS MAY BE MUCH MORE

Same goes for highlighting your work experience. You can possess all the talents in the world, but it won't do the employer any good if you can't do the one thing that she needs you to do, quickly and efficiently.

> Wall Street executive Samuel Walters, 53, was depressed around the holidays because he'd been out of work for eight months. To his great surprise, he was even rejected for a temporary position as a holiday gift wrapper at a national bookstore chain. He could not believe that the young woman who was hiring for the position did not offer him a job. "After all," he kept saying, "I have almost thirty years of Wall Street experience. I can certainly wrap books."

Samuel told me that he went to the bookstore to apply for the position dressed in an expensive business suit. When he spoke to the young woman in charge of hiring, he told her he can certainly wrap gifts, and he then went on at length about his work experience in the financial industry. When I asked Samuel why he wore a suit to the interview, he explained that he'd just left an interview for a Wall Street job that he knew would likely not result in an offer.

I explained to Samuel that, given the dynamics of the loyalty-free workplace, I wasn't surprised that the interviewer didn't hire him. The fact that he worked on Wall Street had no value to her, and his choice of wardrobe didn't help, either. Had he gone to the store dressed modestly in jeans and a dress shirt—and explained he was the father of three children and had wrapped gifts for decades—his chances of landing the job would have been better.

AN INTERVIEW IS NOT THE TIME TO CHANGE A COMPANY

You only have a limited amount of time to spend with a hiring manager, so make the most of it. Don't waste your time talking about how much you know in general. Instead show how much you know about the position they need to fill, and how you can help them fill it.

At the same time, when you're invited to interview for a position, remember that you're a guest—an outsider. By definition, that means, even if you have some knowledge about the company, you have no relationship with it. If you spend part of the interview criticizing the interviewer or the culture of the company, you're not doing yourself any favors.

Lise Poussin, 28, applies for a learning and development position. Lise's resume indicates she worked for a number of French companies and is fluent in French. During the interview, the manager asks Lise whether she is French. Knowing that asking questions about an applicant's national origin should be avoided during an interview, Lise declines to answer because she does not see how that information relates to the position. In addition, she informs the interviewer the asking of that question could subject the company to a workplace discrimination claim.

There is a time and place to protect your employer from problematic business practices. An interview with an employer who hasn't hired you yet, however, is not one of them. In a loyalty-free workplace, you have to be practical if your goal is to land the job. That means knowing when to hold your tongue and when to say your piece.

It would be one thing if Lise were applying for a position in legal compliance, or if the interviewer had directly asked her what she thought of the company's standard interview questions. In either case, highlighting the issue may have been appropriate, though she'd still have to tread carefully to avoid criticizing her prospective employer. But as she was interviewing for a position in learning and development, Lise would have been better off limiting her comments to what she could do to help the company in that capacity.

Remember, companies today are looking for that one perfect candidate. By extension, that means they're looking for reasons to eliminate you from consideration. Don't make their job any easier than it should be.

EMPLOYERS WANT TO SHARE IN THE GAIN, NOT IN THE PAIN

Consider the man who walks into a party with a beautiful woman on his arm. If you're the woman, perhaps you engaged in grueling workouts during the six weeks leading up to the event and did a juice cleanse in order to squeeze into that dress. If you're the man, while you may appreciate all the hard work your partner did to achieve that look, you probably don't want to hear about it. You'd rather just bask in the moment (and watch the others gaze at you with envy) because your partner looks so fabulous.

Along the same lines, employers today want to enjoy the benefits of your hard work. They don't want to hear about the struggles you overcame to get to where you are (because that has nothing to do with them). Nor do they care about your plans for the future (unless they happen to be in sync with their plans).

Alma Laveers, 46, an incredibly talented career counselor, was having trouble moving her career to the next level. She spoke passionately about her upbringing, and specifically of how she had to take care of her younger brothers and sisters at a young age because of her parents' struggles with substance abuse. Though Alma has carried some of these challenges from her childhood into her adult life (including navigating the court system to obtain a permanent restraining order against an abusive ex-husband), she has managed to thrive nonetheless.

It didn't take long for me to see how many people could benefit from Alma's wisdom, no matter where they are in their careers. At the same time, I also understood why she was having trouble landing a new position.

Alma saw her adult struggles and her ability to overcome them as evidence that she could tackle any issue that came her way. A prospective employer, however, would likely view her struggles as evidence of possible ongoing personal issues that could distract Alma from her work (and, quite possibly, cloud her judgment, in the event she's required to manage an employee who is facing similar personal problems). The good news? With some minimal coaching, Alma learned how to convey the relevant information in a way that

> "Business is like oil. It won't mix with anything but business."
>
> **J. GRAHAM**

illustrated how her personal experiences could benefit a future employer, while avoiding any suggestions that her past experiences might hinder her work.

Perspective is everything. If you struggled to put yourself through law school while working three part-time jobs and raising three kids on your own, you probably see yourself as a driven candidate who will let nothing stop you from success. Say that in a job interview, however, and some employers may see your family life as a distraction from your work. Potentially just as damaging, other employers may see you as someone who, given your ambition, expects a fast promotional track within the company, rather than a slow-paced march up the corporate ladder. Similarly, if you tell a prospective employer that you're behind on the mortgage, you might think that would make you a valuable member of the sales team because you're going to be aggressive. But a hiring manager might take that to mean that you're willing to close a deal at any cost in order to earn a commission, regardless of whether that deal is good for the company.

The point is that in the loyalty-free workplace, employers are mostly concerned with finding the perfect fit for any given position. By sharing details about your life that don't relate to your ability to perform the task at hand or to the company's long-term plans, you are providing unnecessary information that could prevent you from landing the job.

> Mindy Anvil, 25, interviews for an executive assistant position that would require her to report to the CEO of a large car dealership. Her past experience as an administrative assistant to a number of senior executives makes her an ideal candidate. When asked where she sees herself in five years, Mindy says that she is looking for an opportunity to grow and develop, and to learn more about the professional opportunities for women in the automotive industry. While Mindy impresses the hiring manager, she does not get the job offer.

After learning about the rejection Mindy reached out to the hiring manager to discuss the company's decision. The manager explained that the CEO was very particular as to how he wants the office run, and therefore was not interested in training someone who would likely be in the job for the short term. Because of this, the company was looking to hire someone with Mindy's skills, but who also saw herself as a career administrative assistant.

That said, one could argue that the hiring manager's thinking was flawed—after all, in the loyalty-free workplace there is no guarantee that anyone will be working for the same employer after three years (let alone five). This applies even to someone whose long-term goal is to become and remain in the same role, such as an executive assistant. However, because they had dozens of other qualified candidates to choose from, the company could afford to be selective.

Along these same lines, while it's good to show some long-term interest in the company during the interview process, don't immediately talk about being promoted or moving to different departments. Wait until you've been hired first.

Now what if you happen to know that it's common for the company to promote from within, perhaps because an internal promotion was the reason for the job vacancy? Assuming it comes up in the interview, you can express an interest in following this path. But if you're interviewing for a teaching position at a university that does not offer tenure, or a non-partnership track position in a law firm where a promotion is not an option, you would be wise in both instances not to bring that up. All that does is tell the interviewer that you're not Cinderella.

SHOW SOME KNOWLEDGE OF THE COMPANY BEFORE YOU GO OUT ON THE INTERVIEW

Job seekers should research a company's culture prior to an interview, so as not to categorize the job in a manner inconsistent with how the company sees it. Going back to our previous example, if you know that the company promotes from within, that tells you that the job for which you're interviewing is probably one with a possibility for advancement. In contrast, if you've seen the same job come up over and over in your job search, that might suggest a problem with turnover—in which case, when discussing future plans, you should focus on the growth opportunities that might exist within the parameters of the vacant role.

In addition, you should walk into the interview with a good idea of the company's business and the products it sells. That means having knowledge of what the company does, the challenges it faces, and any recent news items that may impact its future. On the other hand, that doesn't mean making your personal interest in the job the sole basis for why you should be hired. As is often the case, there's a fine line between showing the right amount of interest, and not enough.

> Social media director Bryson Langer, 31, handles the social media accounts for a large entertainment company. At the suggestion of a family friend, Bryson interviews a bubbly woman, 22, for a vacancy. During their 45-minute meeting, the woman shows Bryson that she has precisely the skills he is looking for. Bryson then asks the applicant what she thinks about the company's growing television network. "I believe that honesty is the best policy," the girl says enthusiastically. "I'm not a fan of the network, but I can learn to love it over time." To no one's surprise, Bryson decides that she is not right for the position.

Employees are representatives of the company. If you want a company to hire you, you need to show them that you have some interest in what they do. If you don't, they'll hire someone else who does.

That said, even if you happen to be a big fan of the company's television network, don't confuse your passion for the network for the knowledge you need to land the job. In fact, while that may seem counterintuitive, in today's climate having too much passion can often work against you.

PASSION IS GOOD, BUT KNOW-HOW IS BETTER

Every year, as graduation season approaches, I love to scour the Internet to read the various commencement speeches given by well-known professionals. With rare exceptions, every speech encourages graduates to "forge ahead, discover your passions, and follow your dreams."

That's an admirable goal, for sure, but it has nothing to do with what it takes to get a job in the loyalty-free workplace.

Now before you start calling me names, let me make an important distinction: A job is an incredibly powerful tool that can help us realize our dreams. Our jobs allow us to make money, which we can use to

> "My father taught me to work; he did not teach me to love it. I never did like to work, and I don't deny it."
>
> **ABRAHAM LINCOLN**

follow our passions, pursue our dreams, and celebrate the things we love. In other words, our jobs and our dreams are *not* one and the same—and yet, far too often, we ignore this reality and try to combine the two.

In the loyalty-free workplace, where companies are fixated on finding candidates with the Cinderella fit, you need to separate your passion from your employment to land the job. There are many practical reasons why. For one, finding work in today's economy is hard enough as it is. Why make it harder on yourself by creating unnecessary obstacles? Yet, if you limit your job search to what you're passionate about, that's exactly what you're doing.

Besides, let's look at the bigger question: Do you know many people who really *love* their jobs? OK, maybe you have a few friends who love the industry in which they work (or, at least, love talking about the fact they work in a particular industry). And if you're like most people, you probably enjoy *some* of what you do at work, and you like enough of your colleagues to consider them friends or even extended members of your family.

> "Why do you think the lottery is so popular? Do you think anybody would play if the super payoff was a job at the night shift in a meat-packing plant?... Like I told you years ago—if work is so good, how come they have to pay us to do it?"
>
> **MIKE ROYKO**
> COLUMNIST

But, when you get down to it, if we really loved everything about our jobs why do we call it work? After all, if you love your job, there's nothing you'd rather do, and no place you'd rather be. But I've had mornings where the *last* thing I wanted to do was get up and go to work (and I'm sure you have, too). And for all the things we like about our job, there are aspects of it that we'd rather not do, and colleagues we could do without seeing.

**"I've tried to be passionate about my career,
but my career just wants to be good friends."**

This is not to suggest that, deep down, we all really hate our jobs. Our jobs are important because they are a means to an end. But they are not, in fact, *the* end. While some people may love what they do for a living, the vast majority of us will never work in jobs for which we have an intense passion, and from which we achieve great joy and satisfaction. That being the case, it makes very little sense to dedicate so much time, energy, and resources to reaching a goal that likely will never materialize. Instead, we're better off looking for positions that match our skills, so that we can obtain the means to enjoy the things that we are passionate about.

ONE'S PASSION MAY NOT ALWAYS TRANSLATE TO ONE'S JOB

Look at it this way. The problem with limiting a job search to jobs that we feel passionate about is that, oftentimes, we don't really know what we might enjoy until we immerse ourselves in it. Not only that, but even if we know what we're passionate about now, how do we know that our passions won't change over time?

Erin Marner, 46, always thought she'd work as a human rights attorney—and after a summer internship at the United Nations, she decided this was her true passion. But, during her third year of law school, she responded to a blog post from a tax professor who was looking for a student to verify the legal citations for an article about the tax implications of tithing. After completing the six-week project, Erin found her contribution acknowledged in the article, which was published in a prestigious tax journal. With law school graduation fast approaching (and having not yet secured a full-time job), Erin used the publicity she received from the article to pursue an associate position in a well-respected law firm that specialized in tax law. Today, Erin is a partner at that firm. While she remains passionate about human rights, she also enjoys her lucrative work as a tax specialist.

Erin may not be passionate about tax law, per se, but she makes a good living at it. Had she limited her job search to positions in human rights, there's no guarantee that she would have enjoyed that work any more than what she currently does, nor earn an income that's close to what she currently makes.

Now let's look at the flip side. What if Erin did find a job in the field of human rights? Would she still be as passionate about that subject if she were immersed in it forty, fifty, or sixty hours a week, week after week, year after year?

Lots of people tell me they are so passionate about the film industry, they'd "do anything to work in it." But, when I mention that I have a friend who manages a database for the sales and leases of movie theaters, they usually say, "That's not what I had in mind." Forget the fact that it's a mid-level contractor/administrator job that directly relates to their stated goal of working in the motion picture industry. Their response indicates that, despite proclaiming that they'd "do anything," they really didn't think that through.

You may have a passion for watching movies, but are you willing to spend sixty hours a week working with challenging personalities, while developing a skin thick enough to deflect the comments of studio executives who think your clients should accept significant pay cuts because they earn too much money?

To be honest, working in the business might even *ruin* your passion for films. There are many retired employees who were once passionate about their jobs—only to never drive a car manufactured by the company from which they just retired, buy a pharmaceutical from the company where they spent the last thirty years working, nor eat at the restaurant that they spent the prior twenty years managing.

I once attended a conference about professional opportunities in the sports field. The audience was filled with passionate sports aficionados—people who could rattle off statistics about different players and games with ease. But for all their knowledge about statistics, very few of these people seemed to know anything about the business of sports. They more likely wanted to be at the games with the players.

There were a lot of successful panelists that day. I don't remember any of them mentioning jobs that would require an employee to know a pitcher's batting average, date of induction into the Hall of Fame, or which coach led the most teams to the Super Bowl. Instead, the esteemed panelists spoke about the intricacies of labor agreements, franchise agreements, merchandising agreements, and archiving certain plays digitally for future viewing upon demand. That data may seem mundane, but it's the sort of information one may need to know if you want to work in the sports industry.

WHEN PASSION CAN WORK AGAINST YOU

Now let's say you've listened to all the arguments and still decide that you will target only those positions that line up with your "dream job." Even so, there are practical reasons why you should discuss your passion only as it relates to the position for which you're interviewing. First, and foremost, despite all your enthusiasm, you may not get the job.

> Toy enthusiast Marisol Soto, 41, interviews for a computer specialist position at a company that manufactures the hottest new toys. To show the company that she is the target audience for the products, Marisol begins the interview by rattling off the names and variations of all of their toys on the market that she has purchased for her children. Then, as the interview progresses, she illustrates that she has the precise skills necessary to perform the job. While the company is impressed with her credentials, they decline to offer Marisol the position because they believe she'd be more interested in the generous discount and other perks that come with the position than the job itself.

In other words, the company felt that Marisol's passion for their line of toys could interfere with her ability to do the job. It would have behooved her to begin the interview by emphasizing her skills first, and her passion second, instead of the other way around.

Instead let's say you interview with someone who thinks your passion is an asset. That still doesn't necessarily mean you'll land the job you want. The company might think that your passion would serve them better if they put you in another position.

> Jeffrey Davis, 38, interviews for a company that represents sports teams. Throughout the interview he speaks of his lifelong interest in hockey, the players, and all of the commercial endeavors related to the sport. The company is impressed with Jeffrey's knowledge of the sports business

and offers him a job—with the understanding that he would not be assigned any clients or duties that directly relate to hockey.

In this situation, while Jeffrey increased his chances of getting hired by mentioning his intense passion for hockey, the company felt that his passion for hockey might interfere with his objectivity when making business decisions. Had he minimized his passion and focused instead on his skills and knowledge of sports business, he would have been more likely to land his "dream job."

PASSION CAN HURT YOU IN THE POCKETBOOK

Finally, no matter how much you love sports, toys, music, or whatever drives your passion, you can't lose sight of the fact that, like everyone else in the loyalty-free workplace, you work for money. If you tell a hiring manager how excited you are to work in their field, he can use your passion against you by offering you a starting salary that is below what the employer originally intended to offer.

After applying for a position as a radio news anchor, Jasmine Bakker, 44, interviews exceptionally well, showing the company that her skills and experience are a perfect fit for the position. The company decides to hire her. Upon accepting their offer, Jasmine immediately tells the company that she is "thrilled to join their team," that it's been her "lifelong dream" to host her own show, and that she'll do whatever it takes to make the show a success. Unbeknownst to Jasmine, the salary she accepted was $10,000 less than what the company had originally budgeted for the position.

Jasmine's situation, unfortunately, is not uncommon. Many employers bank on the fact that there are candidates who will work for less money because of their passion for the job. This is particularly true when it comes to jobs in television and other so-called "dream professions" in the entertainment industry. Employers know that, because many candidates who work in these industries are doing something they love, they're also more willing to work longer hours and take on additional responsibilities without additional compensation.

You may joke with your friends that you love your job at a top fashion magazine so much, you'd work for free. But, when your first child heads off to college, and you realize you have to choose between helping her with tuition or making the maximum contribution to your IRA, you may have a different perspective. The fact is that you should be compensated based

> "The Secret of Success:
> (1) Get a job.
> (2) Get a better job.
> (3) Get an even better job.
> (4) Repeat as often
>   as necessary."
>
> **MATT GROENING**
> CARTOONIST, WORK IS HELL

on the value you bring to your employer, and so you should refrain from unknowingly offering a prospective employer a discount for your services because of your love for the company or the industry.

DON'T LET YOUR BOSS HAVE THE KEYS TO YOUR PASSION

Of course, some job experts scoff at the notion of separating one's passion from the job search/interview process. After all, because we spend most of our adult lives working, it makes no sense to work in a field unless we truly enjoy it. While I understand that argument, it's also beside the point.

This has *not* been a discussion about abandoning your passion. Far from it. Our passions and dreams give us the pleasure and flavor that continue to enrich our lives. I want you to aggressively pursue your passions, and finding a job that will provide you with the financial means to do so is the best way to accomplish this result.

I return to my original distinction: Our jobs are the engines that can drive us to our dreams. The hiring manager—and eventually the person who will become your boss—have the ultimate control over your job. When you equate your job with your dreams and your passions, you're handing someone else the keys to your car. Why would you want to do that?

In the loyalty-free workplace, we have to find out how much companies are willing to pay us to provide the services they want. Each day we cash our paychecks, we can fund whatever it is we love.

If you are still not convinced that this is the best direction, remember that the workplace of today is vastly different than the workplace that used to exist. Because of this, the idea that we should trade in our unrealistic goal of working in a job we love for a more practical job that offers a higher salary is not the only cultural shift. Remember, too, that in the loyalty-free workplace you will not be in your job for an extended period of time.

In the past, it was incredibly important for you to identify your passion and to find a job that was related to it, because it was understood you would be entering into a long-term and mutually beneficial working relationship with your employer. These days, that just doesn't happen. As difficult as it may be to hear, I have to tell you that no one *really* cares about the color of your parachute, your dreams, or your hopes for the future. What prospective employers want to know is whether you can make a contribution to their company and how much they will have to compensate you for that contribution.

And since employees today tend to leave their jobs every three to five years, even if you're currently working in a position that you're not particularly passionate about, that shouldn't make much of a difference because the situation will only last for a short period of time. Your current job is just a stepping stone to your next job, which will offer you *more* compensation, and therefore *more* resources to pursue your lifelong dreams. *This* is something to be truly passionate about.

Remember, as we saw from Erin's example, your passions often develop and change over time, so you should be prepared to change with them. If you want to help the needy, use your income to fund your philanthropy and your time off to work at a soup kitchen. If you love archaeology, use your salary to pay for an online class. If you love movies, find a job that offers you the compensation you need to travel to the Cannes Film Festival. If that doesn't completely fuel your passion (and if you can swing it), finance a film of your own.

Going back to the folks who attended the sports conference, while few of them will probably end up working behind the scenes in sports, all of them had the potential to enjoy extremely lucrative careers in their chosen profession. The income they earned could purchase season tickets, box seats, VIP locker room passes or, in some cases, perhaps even an entire sports team. And if I were to ask them if they'd rather spend their time chasing down the head coach to schedule a personal appearance, or enjoying the benefits of their permanent courtside seats for all home games, I'd imagine most would say the latter.

This should go without saying, but working for money will actually provide you with the money and freedom to satisfy your passions and achieve your personal dreams. The key is to use your short-term commitments to fund your long-term passions.

Remember, in the loyalty-free workplace it's all about the company's needs, and not about yours. We go to work to earn the money and freedom to do the things we want. But to secure that money and freedom, we have to take care of the needs of our employer so that we can do what we want. If you really want to drive the engine of your dreams, remember that success in the workplace begins and ends with your boss. While it's a one-sided relationship in many respects, it's also symbiotic. Remember this is work. There is no loyalty to you and what you need, and there is no place for desperation. The employer's loyalty is to the company and its bottom line, and so to earn your growing and perpetual paycheck you'll have to carefully navigate your relationship with your boss, which is what we'll cover next.

SECRET #2

REMEMBER WHO'S BOSS

Too many people look for jobs that fit their needs. In an age of low unemployment and desperate employers, that may have made sense. But now it's all about the needs of the employer, the company, and, above all, your boss. Today the competition for jobs is fierce. Technology eliminates geographical barriers between employers and prospective applicants because web-based conferencing brings together people from all parts of the world. You need to mold yourself to fit the requirements of job opportunities, rather than wait for opportunities that fit your experiences and desires. If that means playing down your expertise and experience to get the job, so be it.

Then, once you land the job, you have to mold yourself some more to fit the needs and expectations of your boss. If you work for a 68-year-old dinosaur that wears a suit every day and responds only to written memos, you need to dress and play the part. If you're working for a 24-year-old who dresses in jeans and communicates only via text, buy some flip-flops and limber up your thumbs. Whatever your attire, when you make your boss shine, you'll almost immediately see rewards beyond what you ever imagined.

A boss starts his weekly staff meeting by thanking his employees for participating in the recent brainstorming exercises and providing him with constructive feedback on how to improve his management style. He particularly appreciates the suggestion of one particular employee, Eric, that he lighten up and incorporate more humor into his daily interactions with the staff.

Wasting no time, the boss asks Eric to stand.

"Knock, knock," said the boss.

"Who's there?" replies Eric.

"Not you for much longer," says the boss.

—UNKNOWN

Make no mistake about it: Your paycheck and your business card may have the company's name on it, but you work for your boss. He has the power in the relationship—and in the loyalty-free workplace, your success at your job depends on your ability to make that relationship work.

First, your boss has significant control over the terms and conditions of your current employment. He is responsible for completing your performance evaluations, which often serve as the basis for your level of compensation. Most companies will offer you a raise, provided your boss agrees that your work is satisfactory and benefits the company. Conversely, few companies will approve your raise if your boss opposes it.

Second, the more you get along with your boss, the better your chances of advancing your career. Since your boss likely assigns your day-to-day tasks, you'll want to be sure that he has confidence in you and assigns you work of increasing complexity. That way, you will develop skills that make you more marketable for future opportunities, which will enable you to earn enhanced levels of compensation.

Finally, for better or for worse, your reputation at work begins and ends with your boss. How he speaks about your work to others can help or hinder you as you pursue other opportunities. He also may have access to information that you may find useful, not to mention connections to people whose paths you may not otherwise cross.

Navigating one's relationship with the boss requires a practical approach. That can be hard to do sometimes, because it goes against human nature to build relationships with people we may not necessarily like. However, if you really think about it, we often enter into relationships with people, regardless of our personal feelings toward them, because we think we can benefit from that relationship. You may despise a certain real estate broker, but if that broker has the exclusive listings for apartments in a building where you want to live, you'll put your personal feelings aside and work with him. In some cases, we don't recognize the problem until after we've started the relationship. You may have liked your landlord when you signed a one-year lease, only to find him to be meddlesome six months later. Or you may decide, halfway into building a new addition to your home, that you went with the wrong general contractor. In each of these scenarios, you weigh your dissatisfaction with the relationship against the consequences of disrupting it.

Sometimes, though, we may stay in a less than ideal relationship, even if nothing prevents us from leaving it. For example, if your marriage is no longer working, rather than file for divorce right away, you may choose to remain married until your children are grown or your finances are in order. In other words, we muddle through the circumstances for as long as we need to.

> A boss starts out his weekly staff meeting with his regular joke. The entire team started to laugh, except for one employee.
>
> "What's your problem?" asks the boss. "Don't you think I am funny?"
>
> "I no longer have to think you are funny," the employee replies. "Friday is my last day."
>
> —UNKNOWN

Because we work for money and for advancement in the loyalty-free workplace, we do the best we can to earn as much as we can, then move on to whatever is next.

FIGURE OUT HOW YOUR BOSS WORKS

The key to establishing a strong relationship with your boss is to determine what makes that manager tick. A very wise colleague of mine used to remind me, "Sometimes you are the hammer, sometimes you are the nail." Meaning, there will always be instances where your boss will want you to take the lead and complete the project as you see fit. At the same time, there will also be occasions when it's best to fly under the radar and do what your boss says (regardless of whether you agree with him or not).

> "Sometimes you are the hammer, sometimes you are the nail."
>
> **UNKNOWN**

How do you learn the difference? By getting to know your boss' personality and adapting your behavior accordingly. In the loyalty-free workplace, that's what it's all about.

Alexander McKinley, 31, is an employee benefit advisor who is thrilled to have landed a job with a bottling company. On his first day of work, Alexander eagerly shows up a half hour early. Dressed in a pin-striped suit and carrying a briefcase, he waits in the reception area for the others to arrive. The receptionist arrives at 9:00am sharp. Alexander's boss, Lynne Borne, 55, arrives at 9:10am, but as she's late for her 9:00am conference call, she immediately closes her office door. After knocking on Lynne's door, Alexander informs her that he will wait for his first assignment in his office down the hall.

Alexander's employment with the bottling company lasted just seven weeks. Let's just say that his relationship with Lynne went downhill from the moment he arrived. Having come from a corporate environment, Alexander wanted his boss to adapt to

> "A power struggle with your boss is when she has the power and you have the struggle."
>
> ANONYMOUS

his needs, instead of the other way around. That was unfortunate, because he could have averted the entire disaster with a few small modifications.

Alexander lamented Lynne's absence of organization skills and, particularly, her refusal to let him create a simple filing system to track benefit changes. When Lynne asked him to tell her how many benefit complaints were logged in a particular month, he provided her with an itemized spreadsheet that analyzed the type of complaints, when they were filed, and their current status. When Lynne placed Alexander on a performance management plan and told him that his job performance had to improve if he expected to continue to work in the office, Alexander started to work nights and weekends, thoroughly answering emails while copying Lynne on his responses.

It didn't take long for me to peg Lynne's personality: She did not want an organizational system or a detailed spreadsheet, and she certainly didn't want to hear from Alexander on the weekends. Lynne wanted what she wanted when she wanted it, and

> "Don't set your own rules when you are someone's guest."
>
> ITALIAN PROVERB

Alexander should have figured out how to give her what she wanted, in the simplest way possible. When Lynne asked how many complaints were filed, Alexander should have responded with a single number. When she wanted a file, he should have pulled his copy from his own files and handed it to her.

SOME GENERATIONAL GUIDANCE

Need help assessing your boss' style? Here are a few guidelines.

IF YOUR BOSS WAS BORN BETWEEN 1946 AND 1964,
HE IS LIKELY A BABY BOOMER AND THEREFORE

- defines himself by his career, earns a lot of money, and is in a position of authority
- believes hard work produces tangible rewards
- requires "face time," and disapproves of arrangements that permit employees to complete their work from remote locations

IF YOUR BOSS WAS BORN BETWEEN 1965 AND 1980,
HE IS LIKELY A GENERATION Xer, AND THEREFORE

- is independent, self-sufficient, comfortable with technology, and committed to achieving great success—but on his own terms
- is inclined to admit a lack of loyalty to his employer
- sees the importance of a personal life over a career

IF YOUR BOSS WAS BORN IN THE 1980s OR LATER,
HE IS LIKELY A GENERATION Yer (OR CONSIDERS HIMSELF
TO BE A "MILLENNIAL") AND THEREFORE

- is connected to technology 24/7 (and, therefore, prefers to communicate and learn through technology, as opposed to more traditional face-to-face interactions)
- values his personal life over his professional life and will sacrifice rigorous employment situations for a more robust personal life
- is achievement-oriented and expects the company to provide assistance in reaching his goals
- is not afraid to challenge authority
- expects workplace feedback and rewards for his work

Still not sure? Then simply ask your boss what best suits his needs (for example, "Should I give updates as I make progress with a project, or would you rather I update you at our monthly staff meetings?").

If you're like most people, it may take a few interactions before you can appropriately characterize your boss, plus you'll likely gather more information as your relationship evolves. It doesn't matter how you manage to pinpoint his style, so long as you do it.

DON'T TRY TO CHANGE YOUR BOSS—PICK YOUR BATTLES INSTEAD

Let's say you've nailed down your boss' personality, but you still find him difficult to manage. Should you reach out for help? Yes, but tread carefully. In the loyalty-free workplace, there is no guarantee that the process you use or the information you share will remain confidential.

Besides, unless the situation is extreme (such as an issue of safety or discrimination), it's entirely possible that the problem is not with your boss, but with your expectations. Meaning, assuming your boss is an adult with a fully developed personality, certain aspects of his behavior are unlikely to change. In that case, your best bet is to work things out with your supervisor, rather than to go over his head.

Lucinda Alverez, 49, was the assistant manager of a national hotel chain. She worked for the general manager, Brian Curtail, 54. Brian was known for micromanaging his employees and not allowing anyone to make their own decisions. After Lucinda returned from a business trip meeting with the directors of each of the regional offices, Brian summoned her to his office for a full debrief. Lucinda said that she was able to close all of the deals as instructed, "including having the fully executed agreement from the western region, despite the arrogance of that group's director." When Brian asked her to elaborate, Lucinda explained that the director signed the agreement, even though he felt that "corporate greed was taking advantage of the regional centers." Though Lucinda indicated that several other offices expressed similar sentiments, she also told Brian that this was a non-issue.

Before Lucinda knew it, Brian had put his phone on speaker and started dialing the direct line for the director of the western region. Though Lucinda implored Brian not to intervene, he merely waved his hands and told her, "I'll handle it." When the director answered, Brian said, "I have Lucinda Alvarez with me. She tells me you were rude and out of line when you spoke to her. I think you should apologize." The director immediately apologized and insisted that he did not intend to disrespect Lucinda in any way. With that, Brian ended the call and told Lucinda that she did a great job.

Needless to say, Lucinda was completely embarrassed by Brian's actions and wanted my advice on how to handle it. Unfortunately, in a situation like this, where the boss is a fifty-four-year-old middle manager whose penchant for micromanaging is not going to change, the only appropriate response is to make a mental note of it, and move on.

Look at it this way. Being a micromanager, it's Brian's style to get involved with everything. Lucinda knows this, so what did she expect to gain by bringing this to his attention?

"If we want to succeed as a team, we need to put aside our own selfish, individual interests and start doing things my way."

Now, let's say that, after the phone call to the western region, Lucinda told Brian that she wished he would've handled the situation differently. Best case, Brian would have actively listened to Lucinda's concerns and altered his future behavior. The problem is, being a micromanager Brian would have also felt compelled to do something about it such as picking up the phone, making another call to the western director, and trying to undo the situation. All that would have done was make Lucinda even more embarrassed.

You'll notice that I did not suggest that Lucinda just move on—instead, I suggested she make a mental note of it and move on. After all, her embarrassment aside, the situation actually provided a wealth of information that Lucinda can use to her advantage. For one, she now knows that, if she doesn't want Brian to be involved in a particular matter, she should keep it to herself. Conversely, if she does want him to intervene, all she has to do is say it. More to the point, Lucinda also now knows that Brian likes her work. Whatever she's doing, she should keep doing

it. Remember this is a boss-employee relationship and therefore, by definition, it is about her boss. Lucinda now basically has a road map as to how Brian will handle what he sees as inappropriate behavior. It is not up to Lucinda to change his response; instead it is up to Lucinda to modify her behavior in response to it.

HOW DO YOU HANDLE A NARCISSISTIC BOSS? BY MANAGING UP

In the loyalty-free workplace, you have to keep your boss happy. That can be tricky if your boss happens to be a narcissist. After all, to a narcissist, everything is about them—you can't expect them to reward you for your accomplishments, no matter how hard you try.

WHEN YOU MANAGE UP, YOU MOVE UP.

Yet, even a narcissistic boss can be handled successfully, so long as you separate yourself from the narcissistic personality. Meaning, if a narcissist subjects you to unwarranted harsh criticism, remember the harshness is more about them than it is about you. One effective way to effectively manage this situation is to manage up.

Managing up simply means to work according to this credo: "When the boss looks good, you look good." By making your boss look good, you establish trust and good will with him. Therefore, anything that reflects favorably on your boss will reflect favorably on you.

> A boss takes his employee for a ride in his new car.
>
> "Wow! This is an amazing car," says the employee.
>
> "It certainly is," says the boss. "And if you exceed this year's goals more than you exceeded last year's goals, then next year I will get an even better one."
>
> —UNKNOWN

The fact is, when you manage up, you make yourself indispensable to your boss. That can provide you with some degree of job security as you look for your next opportunity.

RESPECT THE ROLE

To effectively manage up, you have to understand that your job is to help your boss with his work, and not create more work for him by being difficult to manage.

Ana Bellingers, 23, is a recent college graduate. While dining out with her parents, Ana is asked whether she will have trouble getting time off for her cousin's upcoming out-of-town wedding. "Of course not," she replies. "This is my cousin's wedding, so I am going. I don't need to ask my boss for time off. I just need to inform her that I will be out of the office."

Being a typical Millennial, Ana tends to value her personal life over her professional life. That's fine if she happens to work for herself—but she doesn't. She has a boss, and she needs to remember that if she wants to keep her job and keep herself in the best position to increase the size of her paycheck.

> "A company hires you to resolve company problems, not to be the problem of the company."
>
> **UNKNOWN**

In the loyalty-free workplace, your boss is still your boss, and you have to respect their role. That means reporting to work on time, requesting permission to work different hours if you have a doctor's appointment, and asking for approval if you want certain days off. That also means making your boss' life as easy as possible. Your boss doesn't want to walk into the office wondering whether you're going to do your job that day, or if he still has a customer base because he hired you.

I once received a call from a very successful dentist who asked if I knew anyone who might be interested in working as an office manager. When I asked him about the qualifications for the position, he said, "All I want is someone who will show up to work on time." When I asked if he could expand on that, he explained that while all of his prior office managers came highly recommended, they each also ended up hurting his business, despite being good at their job. In one case, the manager had a habit of sharing too much information. For example, one day she called in sick.

> "Don't broadcast your troubles. There's no market for them."
>
> **UNKNOWN**

When she returned to work the following day, the dentist asked how she was feeling. The manager proceeded to tell him at length about how her virus was related to her stomach problems, vomiting, and what she'd been eating for the past two days. Unfortunately for the dentist, this exchange happened to take place in the reception area, in front of several waiting patients.

Does this mean that you should never share any personal issues with your boss? Not necessarily. You are only human and you will likely want to establish some type of personal connection. But there's a time and a place for everything. If your boss asks you to get Mrs. Klein's x-rays, or is waiting for you to format the PowerPoint slides for his upcoming presentation to the board of directors, the last thing he wants to hear at that moment is about your break-up, financial difficulties, problems with the mover, or what you had for dinner last night that made you so terribly sick.

Remember your boss has a job to do, too. While managing you is part of that job, it shouldn't take up so much of his time that it prevents him from getting his own work done. If it does, he will find someone else.

Does managing up mean you should be a brownnoser or a sycophant? No. But it does mean equipping your boss with the information he needs to do his job effortlessly and effectively. Remember, by making your boss look indispensable, you've made yourself indispensable, too.

Now what if your boss has a reputation for being unprepared in meetings, or does not come across well or command any respect? That could reflect poorly on you. If this is the case, it's even more imperative that you manage up. By looking out for your boss, you are also looking out for yourself. In the loyalty-free workplace, no one is going to reach out to you and give you a reward. If you want to be acknowledged, you have to assert your relevance to your boss and, when practical, to others around you.

BE PROACTIVE: ANTICIPATE YOUR BOSS' NEEDS

Another benefit of managing up: By showing others that you and your boss can handle challenging tasks, they will not only value your expertise, but know that they can rely on you to get the work done with little to no interference. Your boss will appreciate that, because it shows he knows how to manage effectively to produce impressive results. But that also benefits you by providing a semblance of job security, even in a loyalty-free workplace. For example, in the event the company faces reorganization that will include layoffs, your boss will keep your name out of those conversations—if only because it's in *his* best interest to ensure you remain at his side.

> **"Above all, be loyal to your superior's agenda."**
>
> **JOHN DELOREAN**
> BUSINESSMAN SUMMARIZING THE CORPORATE PHILOSOPHY OF ROGER SMITH, CEO OF GENERAL MOTORS

Remember, the best employees manage themselves—they report to work on time and are where they need to be. Along the same lines, prospective employers can usually gauge what type of employee you might be during the interview process. If you show up for the interview on time and ready to go, you stand a much better chance of getting hired than someone who needs to reschedule an interview three times, or who arrives late or unprepared.

Say you have a friend who is coping with an aging parent or a seriously ill child. If you're like most people, you may send flowers or tell them, "Anything you need, just ask." While those gestures are certainly appreciated, the ones that really stand out are when you empty your friend's dishwasher and take out the trash.

You should approach your relationship with your boss in much the same way. Besides making yourself easy to manage, let your boss know that you're ready to help when he needs it—and act on it when he asks. If she's overwhelmed with an upcoming presentation, offer to draft some of the more mundane parts of the presentation, or perhaps to format the slides. Even if she says no, she will remember that you were willing to support her when she needed it. That will serve you well in the end.

SMARTER IS BETTER

What if you think you're more qualified than your boss, or believe you deserve some of the credit that he receives? For one, this is not a bad place to be, and you wouldn't be alone—many successful executives hire team members who are smart and talented, especially in areas where they do not excel, because they know they can make them shine. That being the case, it becomes even more imperative that you manage up. After all, since your boss has no loyalty, he is less likely to support you as his career takes off if he knows you're not there for his best interests—whereas, when your boss knows you're there for him, he might tell the senior executives that you're the best person to succeed him in his current position when he leaves for another company. It could also mean creating a spot for you at a higher level when he moves to another company and is charged with hiring a new team.

> "Always be smarter than the people who hire you."
>
> **LENA HORNE**

This brings us to another point. Part of managing up is learning about the goals of your boss and helping him achieve them. Not only will that cement your relationship, it will help your boss earn a promotion which, in turn, can help you advance your career.

The same holds true for issues related to compensation. Whether you like your boss or can't stand him, it's in your best interest to help him earn a raise. If your boss gets a raise, you'll likely get one, too. But if his salary is frozen because he's on a performance management plan, guess what? Your chances for a salary increase will likewise be affected.

And when the time comes to ask for a raise (or any other personal request), don't just say, "I'd like more money every week." Instead, phrase it in a way that makes it seem like you're helping your boss as well. If you need to earn a certain level of income in order for the job to be an option (or would like the company to pay for a course in continuing education), emphasize the skills that you bring to work every day and how that will continue to benefit the company. Similarly, if you need to adjust your work schedule because of personal obligations, present the request in terms of how this will "maximize your productivity at the office."

ENOUGH ABOUT YOUR BOSS, MORE ABOUT YOUR BOSS

In the loyalty-free workplace, a shrewd employee can get what he wants so long as the employer also gets what *they* want in return.

> Bob Ashwell, 36, works for a company that is hosting a retreat to celebrate the launch of a new bicycle. As part of his job, Bob is expected to lead one of the groups through a bike tour. The weekend before the convention Bob breaks his ankle and will therefore be unable to participate in the ride.
>
> Bob's boss decides to replace him at the retreat with another employee who was not originally scheduled to attend. Bob strenuously objects to his boss' decision to exclude him from the event and wants to discuss the matter further.

Even though he couldn't lead the bike ride as previously planned, Bob still wanted to attend the retreat because he saw it as a valuable opportunity to network with staff members from other parts of the country. Just as important, he was concerned that his absence from the event would reflect badly on him at the office. To resolve the situation, he prepared a memo to his boss outlining the reasons he felt it was important for him to be there.

First, Bob explained he planned to meet with a number of people at the convention to resolve some challenging issues that, for one reason or another, had stalled. Many of these matters involved personnel from other regional officers who were attending the event. By meeting these parties face to face, Bob felt that he could resolve these matters efficiently, without the company incurring the costs of multiple overnight trips. In addition, knowing that the company would have a business office set up for use by the attendees, Bob offered to relieve the administrative assistant of her responsibilities during the bike tour—that way, he could oversee the office, while the administrative assistant led the bike ride.

After reviewing the memo, Bob's boss reconsidered his decision and permitted Bob to attend the event within the parameters he outlined. The key for Bob was identifying his needs first, and then presenting them in a manner that met the needs of his employer.

> Advertising executive Ann Garrity, 37, is about to return from her maternity leave. Though she knows that she is a valued employee, her company is facing a one-year wage freeze. Ann would like to work from home at least one day a week so that she can spend more time with her newborn and avoid the grueling 70-mile daily commute. She is about to discuss these matters with her boss, but does not believe her scheduled call will go well.

Ann first came to me with the idea of changing jobs. After a brief discussion, we both agreed that it would be better for her if she remained in her current position with new terms, at least for the time being. The question was how to broach the matter with her boss.

Ann's initial plan was to be very direct—she wanted to work from home to spend more time with her children and less time commuting to and from work. In other words, "This is my need, and this is what benefits me." The problem with that approach, of course, is twofold. If her employer is like most companies, they will probably worry that if she works from home, any time she spends with her baby may impair her ability to do her job. And as for her commuting costs, her boss will likely tell Ann, "That's your problem, not mine."

However, with a few adjustments, Ann presented her request in a way that benefited her *and* her employer. For one, she said that she'd agree to the one-year salary freeze in exchange for working from home twice a week. This arrangement would offset the money she'd need to continue to fill her gas tank. In addition, knowing that the company recently rented office space on another floor to accommodate the growing staff, she suggested that she share her office with another employee who is offered a similar arrangement. That would save the company the additional cost of at least one office on another floor.

Not only did Ann's boss accept this arrangement, but he applauded her for coming up with a creative way of address-ing the company's financial pressures without impacting any of its clients. While Ann's

"Office politics is just like the lottery. Dreaming about winning doesn't get you anywhere—there's no payoff if you don't buy a ticket. You have to play if you want to win.**"**

JAMIE FABIAN

income won't grow for the next twelve months, she will save money in commuting costs every month, not to mention spare herself of six hours of driving per week—time that she can spend with her family, or looking for her next job.

Now, you may ask, "If it's all about addressing the needs of the boss, aren't we being disingenuous when we seek out mutual benefits?" The answer to that is no. After all, employers engage in the same behavior all the time in the loyalty-free workplace. A wise employee keeps that in mind when discussing the terms and conditions of employment.

I once had a client who landed a coveted job at a large power company. He was quite proud of the fact that he was assigned the largest office in the building, which included a plush couch, a private bathroom, and even his own shower. Naturally, he saw those perks as an indication of how much the company valued him. What he didn't realize was that, by lavishing him with the comforts of home, the company was expecting him to put in longer days at the office. Why bother going home to get a few hours of sleep and a shower, when he could merely take a quick nap in his office, shower, and be ready to go back to work?

Few people would ever agree to work twenty-hour days. But you might be more willing to spend many more nights at the office (as this client did), if it meant getting a large office with your own bathroom in return.

The point is, when you manage up, you can put yourself in a position to advance your career, while also making your boss shine.

NEVER TAKE A JOB BASED ON WHO YOU THINK YOU'LL BE WORKING FOR

So far we've talked about how to handle an actual boss. Now let's take a look at how to handle a prospective boss.

What if you learn that you're about to be reassigned to the proverbial Boss from Hell—a complete jerk who goes through assistants like Kleenex because he runs them ragged? Do you start sending out resumes or call your friend the recruiter? Or what if you've interviewed for a position that seems like a perfect fit—you meet the qualifications, the work atmosphere is friendly and easygoing, and the boss is an absolute dream?

In both scenarios, you have to remember that the rules of the loyalty-free workplace apply to everyone. No one's tenure is any more guaranteed than yours. Therefore, whether your prospective boss has a fantastic reputation or a lousy one, you should never base an employment decision on for whom you *think* you'll be working. Why? Because the people to whom you're actually reporting can change at a moment's notice.

A single mom stuck in a dead end job with a government agency, Marnie Maynard, 31, interviewed for a position with a non-profit agency. Many people warned her about the excessive red tape at the organization, and that her prospective boss was known to be a very unstable woman. When she interviewed, however, Marnie found that, due to a reorganization, she would be reporting to the head of the department—a man who was not only well-respected, but could be an invaluable resource. The red tape, however, was not an exaggeration. Though Marnie originally interviewed for the position in November, it would be four months before she finally received the job offer in March. She would not start in the new position until May 1st.

Unfortunately for Marnie, on her first day of work, she learned that the man who was supposed to be her boss was reassigned to a new position.

Naturally, Marnie was distraught—especially once she learned that the new head of the department was the very same woman that she had been told to avoid. However, just two months later, she had a happy ending: The troublesome woman resigned, leaving Marnie with an entirely different job and reporting structure than what had been originally contemplated. The point is, nothing in the loyalty-free workplace is guaranteed. That goes for the benefits of the position (such as continued job security) and the drawbacks (a less than ideal boss).

BEWARE OF INFORMATION FROM THIRD PARTIES

Remember, too, that everyone puts his best foot forward during an interview, including the interviewer. So even if you develop a bond with a potential boss during the interview process, that may not reflect how she would behave in other situations. Further, even if your prospective boss seems incredibly inspiring during the interview process, she may not be as inspiring when handling her daily supervisory responsibilities.

Besides, what you hear about a prospective boss may not reflect reality. As the saying goes, no matter how flat you make a pancake, it still has two sides.

David Aarons, 26, is a recent law school graduate looking for a job. He has heard many horror stories about law firm partners who torment their junior associates as part of the process to initiate them into the practice of law. After interviewing with one law firm partner, David sees no red flags but is taken aback by the candor of the two other associates who speak to him as part of the interview process. Both junior associates tell David that the partner is difficult to work with, and they recount situations where they received emails in the middle of the night, with aggressive deadlines that came and went even before they woke up to read the original email.

They also speak of being chastised in large group meetings, low employee morale, and the high turnover rate (which they say accounts for the current vacancy).

David then speaks with a law school career counselor who emphasizes the importance of finding a first job in a supportive environment. Based on that conversation, David decides not to work at that particular law firm, even before learning whether an offer would have been made.

Not only did David opt out of the interview process without even knowing the terms of any offer he might have received (or even confirming what supervisory structure might have been in place), he based his decision on the input of two employees with whom he had no prior history.

Most employees know better than to speak negatively of their supervisors, particularly at a time when their current income depends on the continuation of that relationship. For all David knew, these two associates may have been so distraught over their current employment status that they no longer cared about their utter lack of professionalism.

Then again, one imagines that the associates may have had some ulterior motivations for sharing negative information with David. (As it happens, a few years after that interview, David learned that the firm filled the position by hiring an associate that had previously worked for the firm.) While there's no way to confirm this, it's entirely possible that the two associates had another friend whom they wanted to see hired instead of David—in which case, it would have been in their best interest to dissuade David, and any other candidates, from pursuing the job. It's also possible, given the competitive nature of the loyalty-free workplace, that the associates simply viewed the hiring of an additional associate as a threat to their future employment.

> "No matter how flat you make a pancake, it still has two sides."
>
> **DR. PHIL**

The point is, third parties in the interview process—that is to say, people whom you may meet in the course of the interview, but who have no bearing whatsoever in the final decision—may act in a way to impact the process. Your job is to determine whether they're giving you useful information, or not. What's the difference? Useful information is that which ultimately helps you achieve your end goal, which is to earn a growing and perpetual paycheck.

Let's consider another example:

> Madeline Deveer, 42, applied for a job as a patient service representative at a large city hospital. After meeting with her prospective boss (who had no reservations about Madeline's ability to work for her), Madeline met with several other hospital employees as part of the interview process. One employee, Edwin Gainer, 36, suggests that Madeline's prospective boss would be challenging to work with. Although Edwin did not provide any additional details, it was clear to Madeline that he was discouraging her from taking the job. Though Madeline gave Edwin's comments some thought, when she was offered the position—at a salary that was considerably higher than her current job—and she accepted the offer.
>
> Madeline ended up thriving in her new position and established an excellent rapport with her boss.

When Madeline accepted the position, she did not know any specific details about the relationship between Edwin and her future boss. But, as far as Madeline is concerned, it didn't matter. Her only goal is the same as yours: to maintain a stream of income and, ideally, to increase that stream of income over time. Of course you want to enter into a new situation with your eyes open, but *you* want to be the one making the decision.

It turned out that four years after Madeline started working for the company, she learned that her boss and Edwin had once been romantically involved, and that their relationship ended badly. This certainly explained the feelings of animosity Edwin may have had toward her boss. Even still, had she known that information at the time the offer was presented, it still should not have had any impact on her decision.

> "The handwriting on the wall may be a forgery."
>
> RALPH HODGSON
> ENGLISH POET

Remember, the ultimate goal is to get a promotion that offers you more compensation. If working at the hospital for Edwin's former girlfriend helps Madeline reach that goal, then she should accept the offer. If it doesn't, then she should look for the next opportunity.

Along the same lines, just as you should never dismiss a great opportunity because of the potential for a terrible boss, don't be afraid to pursue opportunities for advancement (and a larger paycheck), no matter how amazing your current boss is. In the loyalty-free workplace, you must always look out for yourself.

Gary Anderson, 56, works as an architect in a corporate development firm. Gary performs a lot of work behind the scenes, for which his boss, Lenny Hart (also 56), receives credit. In return, Lenny uses his influence to ensure that Gary receives challenging work and significant salary increases.

When Gary is approached by a recruiter about a ground-floor opportunity at a new firm that offers a significant salary increase, he declines to even meet with the recruiter to discuss the position, out of loyalty to Lenny. Six months later, however, Lenny announces he is leaving the company to work for a competing development firm. When Lenny's replacement is hired, he has a new vision for the department. As a result, Gary finds himself out of a job.

In this case, Gary lost sight of the reason for all of his hard work: to qualify for promotional opportunities. At the very least, he should have talked to the recruiter about the new opportunity, even though accepting it would have required him to leave the solid working relationship he had developed with Lenny. Besides, if Gary could successfully "manage up" one boss, he should be able to do the same with the next one.

> "Would I ever leave this company? Look, I'm all about loyalty. In fact, I feel like part of what I'm being paid for here is my loyalty. But if there were somewhere else that valued loyalty more highly, I'm going wherever they value loyalty the most."
>
> **DWIGHT SCHRUTE**
> FROM THE TELEVISION SHOW THE OFFICE

No doubt, there are incredible bosses, just as there are terrible bosses. But all bosses have to make tough decisions sometimes, especially in the loyalty-free workplace. Gary may have loved Lenny, but if Lenny had been forced to lay Gary off while he was still paying college tuition for his two children, he may think differently.

Remember, too, that because the workplace is loyalty-free, at some point your boss may have to make decisions that are in his best interest and perhaps not in yours. Say you're in the break room, having an animated conversation with a coworker. You raise your voice and make an innocuous comment in jest. The coworker, however, feels threatened by your comment, and files a formal complaint. Even though the boss knows that you were just being funny (and doesn't see you as a threat at all), depending on the circumstances, he may have to impose disciplinary action.

This goes back to the point we made in our earlier example with Marnie: Never make a workplace decision based on your current boss. In the loyalty-free workplace, that sort of information can change on a moment's notice (as Gary learned the hard way).

YOU CAN'T CONTROL ANY MOVEMENT OTHER THAN YOUR OWN

In a loyalty-free workplace, there are no guarantees. We can't expect any aspect of our employment, or that of our boss or coworkers, to remain the same. All we can do is work as best we can in the circumstances in which we find ourselves, no matter what those circumstances are.

While this may seem daunting at first, it really isn't once you stop and think about it. After all, everyone is in the same boat, and the tide can turn before you know it. Knowing that, a smart employee will continue to earn his perpetual and growing paycheck by accepting the importance of getting along with his boss, whoever that is, at any given time.

When you manage up, you move up. Once you master how that works, it will not matter who your boss is, because you'll know that you can successfully implement this strategy over and over again. Keep in mind that even if you are effectively managing your boss, the rewards may not be immediate. In fact, it is inevitable that there will be times when you do not receive the results you desire, or that it will seem like everyone else is moving upward and onward and you are standing still. The good news is that even when you are faced with what seems like a dire situation, there are almost always hidden benefits that can be easily claimed. This is the focus of secret number three.

TURN TROUBLES INTO TRIUMPHS

As you navigate the workplace, you must always focus on your main goal: earning and growing your perpetual paycheck. This will not always be easy, since today's work environment is objectively difficult and no one is immune from its hardships and heartaches. Yet, more often than not, even the most difficult situations can present opportunities to boost your income.

The business world is filled with examples of forward-thinking entrepreneurs who made their millions by seeing crises as launching pads for future profits. Google, for one, earns close to $500 million a year by placing advertisements on the websites people land on after having mistyped a letter or two in the name of the website they initially intended to visit.

> "Things turn out best for the people who make the best of the way things turn out."
>
> JOHN WOODEN

Let me give you a personal example. I have fond memories of a birthday dinner as a young child, when my parents told me I could invite eight of my closest friends to a "grown-up" dinner at one of my favorite chain restaurants. My family, friends, and I all congregated in the vestibule of the restaurant more than fifteen minutes before the time of our guaranteed reservation for a party of thirteen, only to find ourselves still waiting for our table almost two hours later. As soon as the conversations turned to vows to never return, two managers entered the vestibule clapping their hands, playing kazoos, and singing "Happy Birthday" to me as they wheeled out a tray of appetizers for us to sample. The presentation was a memorable event, which we talked about for weeks, the highlight of which was the free appetizers. The two-hour delay was never mentioned.

The point is, everyone in business is looking for a way to convert wrongs into rights and obstacles into steps forward. Even when things don't go well at work, with the right mindset you can still turn a trouble into a triumph and pave the way for future success.

Consider the classic story of two shoe salesmen who traveled to an under-developed area in Africa and found that no one in the area was wearing any shoes. The salesmen immediately sent simultaneous emails back to their corporate headquarters. The first man wrote, "This trip is a waste of time—no one wears shoes!" The second man wrote, "Double the original order. The demand will be at least twice what we originally expected!"

Then there's Frank W. Abagnale, the well-known con artist whose life was chronicled in the Steven Spielberg film *Catch Me If You Can* (based on Abagnale's best-selling book of the same name). Frank cashed $2.5 million in fraudulent checks in every state and twenty-six foreign countries. After being captured and serving five years in various prisons, Frank was released, provided that he assist the federal government with their fraud detection work. Instead of view-ing himself as an unemployed man with a criminal record with little chance of

> "The pessimist complains about the wind. The optimist expects the wind to change. The realist adjusts the sails."
>
> **WILLIAM A. WARD**

finding a job, Frank converted the legally mandated relationship into a fraud prevention business that has now spanned close to forty years, providing the gold standard for more than 14,000 corporation and law enforcement agencies.

Remember the words of Winston Churchill: "Difficulties mastered are opportunities won." Put another way, how you characterize something impacts how you respond to it. Labeling an event as a problem compels you to adopt a negative approach, whereas labeling it as an opportunity compels you to adopt a positive approach. Positive people continue to move forward regardless of what is happening. Negative people use whatever is happening around them as a justification for remaining in the same place, moving backward, or moving in the wrong direction. Viewing workplace changes as opportunities for growth increases the chances that you will uncover ways to produce significant rewards.

Workplace changes are stressful, unsettling, and may cause you to re-examine your place and purpose. These changes often have a domino effect, causing decreased morale and depression at a time when employees are asked to not only continue with their work, but produce even better results. When faced with any of these changes, rather than pull back and exert the minimal amount of work necessary to collect your paycheck, try seeing these crises as opportunities. In most cases, by stepping up you'll put yourself in a position to reap immediate rewards, such as new titles or roles, before anyone else.

Let's look at some commonly perceived workplace crises and the significant opportunities each situation presents.

"I'M SORRY, WE'RE GOING TO HAVE TO LET YOU GO."

The moment you're told this, you must accept the fact that this particular job has come to an end and you must find a new position. Unsettling, yes, but look at the bright side: Countless others with much less experience and fewer skills than you have been in this same position and prevailed. As of the time this book went to press, there are four million open jobs in the United States. You only need one. The odds are certainly in your favor! Second, regardless of how dire your circumstances may be, there is a job for you. You just have to find it. There are jobs out there for *everyone*.

Check out these positions:

- *Chicken sexter:* friendly individual needed to get up close to baby chicks to separate them according to sex.
- *Odor tester:* chemist needed to ensure that deodorants really do prevent offensive odors.
- *Dice swallower:* adventurous eater needed for 18ᵗʰ century English gambling den whose sole responsibility will be to swallow the dice in the event of a police raid.
- *Ostrich babysitter:* watch person needed to keep an eye on the ostriches to ensure they are not stolen and do not peck each other to death.
- *Therieogenologist:* board-certified medical doctor specializing in animal reproduction needed to assist with the artificial insemination of bulls.

OK, so perhaps these jobs are not exactly what you have in mind. My point is, there's a job for everyone. All you need to claim that job is an immediate and concrete action plan. Keep in mind that as soon as you are let go, many of the circumstances that might have been standing between you and great success are no longer an issue.

If you were looking for the motivation to move your career to the next level, now you have it. It is easy for a job search to get pushed further down on a priority list, as other matters that "cannot" wait move further up on the list. No more excuses, no more discussions about failed efforts to follow up on a particular lead or to reach out to an old colleague. You lost your job. The time is *now.*

Even though you may not be looking forward to the upcoming job search, you do have something positive to look forward to: a new job with new rewards. You likely need a new job and source of income to survive, so now you have a very limited amount of time to figure it out and find your next opportunity. Finding a new job is no

> "The ultimate inspiration is a deadline."
>
> NOLAN BUSHNELL

longer something you want to do, or daydream about doing. Instead, finding a new job is a very clear, specific, and targeted goal that must be achieved.

Last week you may have been depressed about the notion that you would be in a dead-end job for another year, without any appreciation or hope for advancement. Now you can take comfort in knowing you will no longer be stuck in this rut, and that at this time next year you will be working for a new employer, with different people, and heading in a new direction.

British historian and author Cyril Northcote Parkinson famously theorized that "work expands so as to fill the time available for its completion." If you have a general notion that you want to find a job in the next one to two years, you will find a job in the next one to two years. However, if your employment ends and you only have enough money in your emergency fund to support yourself for one or two months, you will inevitably find a new job in the next one to two months. It is human nature to devote a degree of effort to a task that is commensurate with the time you have available to achieve it. Given a shorter time to find a new job, your motivation increases and results are achieved at a faster pace.

Some other good news is that concerns about not having the time to dedicate to your search are now gone. You no longer have to worry about a micro-manager who tracks your every move. Mid-afternoon interviews in remote locations are no longer an issue. Interviews no longer need to be scheduled before work or during lunch. You do not have to keep claiming you have yet another doctor's appointment for an undiagnosed ailment. No more speedy clothing changes in the restroom from your casual work clothes to your interview suit. Now your time is your own. You are free, agreeable, and accommodating—the precise traits employers in the loyalty-free workplace look for when hiring new employees.

You now also have time to do whatever needs to be done to transition to a new industry or into a new role. Haven't had the time to attend those conferences to network and meet the right decision-makers? Now you do. Haven't had the time to sign up for those preparatory classes, certifications, and go back to school? Dust off those registration forms and go. Now you can tackle the list of people you want to reach out to for lunch or for coffee to talk about new opportunities in their company or to explore career options. Maybe you wanted to apply for jobs at a higher level, but needed to get some additional training, or an advanced degree. You are now one step closer to that goal because your calendar has freed up and you have the time necessary to put those plans into place.

Lots of job seekers tell me they just need a few weeks of paid time off to formulate and execute their job search plans. If you have unused vacation days that your employer will pay out, or you are receiving a severance package, that extra money can buy the time you'll need to do just that.

If you are provided a few weeks of "working notice" in advance of your end date, you can also use that time to put your search into high gear. Of course, you will likely have obligations to help with the transition and you will want to cooperate in that regard. But now that your exit is inevitable, you can stop exerting extra efforts. Feel free to schedule lunch meetings that you previously thought too lengthy. Go ahead and schedule early morning meetings and meetings immediately after work. If this situation means

> "If at first you don't succeed,
> find out if the loser gets anything."
> **WILLIAM LYON PHELPS**

coming in a few minutes late or leaving a few minutes early, it's unlikely to be a significant issue. Make and take telephone calls freely. You no longer need to worry that your boss will overhear you speaking with a recruiter. Now that you have a time-certain end date, you can start to schedule multiple meetings on the days that will follow the end of your employment. If you receive two weeks of working notice, set a goal to have ten meetings set up by the time your employment ends. That way, on your first day off work you will already have things scheduled.

If in the past people suggested conferences you should attend or courses you should take, calendar those activities. If you are implementing the advice given to you by a specific person, circle back with that person to provide an update. An email reminding them of the advice provided and confirming that you are heeding that advice is a great way of informing them you are looking for a new opportunity and appreciate their keeping you in mind for suitable positions.

All of these plans can become an integral and powerful part of your upcoming job search discussions and networking meetings. When a prospective employer asks you about your goals, you can tell them that you will be leaving your employment on a certain date to complete the training and gain experience that is aligned with your future goals—which, coincidentally, are related to the position for which you are interviewing.

Prospective employers are inundated with job seekers talking about their interest in changing industries or transitioning into new roles. Based on the intense competition for employment, employers understandably question whether the expressed interest is genuine. Job seekers can easily prove their seriousness by outlining the details of their plans that are already in place. For example, if you're a shoe salesman seeking to use your transferable customer service skills to work in banking, you can tell a prospective bank employer that you're currently enrolled in a class about the variety of banking products that can be incorporated into a customer's financial plan. Similarly, if you're a criminal attorney who wishes to become a teacher, and you happen to be scheduled to present a continuing education class at the local bar association, that also shows employers that you are committed to your new, desired field. Not only that, you're adding skills that can increase your marketability while also expanding your network, which might provide valuable connections as your job search continues. That is precisely what happened to Charles English.

Banking attorney Charles English, 55, wanted to spend his final 10 years of employment working as an arbitrator before eventually retiring, but he grew increasingly frustrated with his stalled transition. Most work in this field is assigned to arbitrators with decades of experience, making it difficult for others to break into the field. Compounding the challenge, Charles learned that, to even appear on a list of eligible decision-makers, he must demonstrate a certain number of successful resolutions. Not only that, but in some cases, to obtain the experience needed to be eligible even for consideration, he would have to resign from his current position.

Though Charles knew of a number of pro bono programs that would offer him the opportunity to serve as an arbitrator (and therefore obtain the experience he needed), he'd always declined to participate; as much as he wanted to become an arbitrator, he could not afford to make that sort of significant time commitment for no remuneration. But, when he was given notice that his employment would end, Charles realized this was an ideal opportunity to revisit his plan to become an arbitrator. Within a few days of learning of his impending layoff, he reached out to the coordinator of the pro bono program to let her know of his upcoming availability, and he scheduled pro bono work to begin on the first day of his unemployment. He also reached out to the administrators of a number of different rosters and let them know that he expected to have met the basic minimum training minimum requirements in the near future. He asked if they could expedite the review of his application to determine his eligibility.

It turned out that Charles received an added benefit from this pro bono opportunity. Yes, it provided him with some basic training on how to manage certain hearings. But since three practitioners were assigned to each hearing, each assignment provided him with the opportunity to meet two other people working in the field. In many cases, those people were well-established practitioners who offered him valuable advice as to how to build a successful practice of his own. The program also held semi-annual networking sessions, during which he was able to continue to expand his network and learn from others.

The outcome? Rather than telling prospective clients that he was laid off from a law firm due to lack of work, Charles was able to say that he left his position as a prominent attorney to make the transition to becoming an arbitrator, and that he was working in a pro bono program as he made that transition. Had Charles not been laid off, he might have never made the transition to what has become a very successful arbitration practice.

"EVERYONE AROUND ME IS BEING TERMINATED OR LAID OFF."

Your company is going through a round of layoffs. Some of your friends have been laid off. Some people in your department have been let go. And a few other people from around the company were also terminated. You're afraid that you could be next.

Keep in mind that while others may have been laid off or terminated, you have not. You still have your job, your paycheck, and your benefits. Regardless of what may be happening around you, it hasn't happened to you—at least, not yet.

Also, keep in mind that employers spend significant money and resources to attract and retain their employees. As such, it is unlikely an employer will terminate or lay off an employee for no reason at all. Aside from the time, money, and resources needed to replace the departed employee, employers know that costly litigation may result from layoffs executed for inappropriate reasons. Also, having a reputation for hasty terminations can hurt an employer's ability to recruit and retain top talent. Finally, while not blaming the victim, odds are the impacted employees knew (or at least should have known) that their employment was coming to an end and should have made at least some minimal preparations for the transition.

I am not saying you are completely in the clear. You now have first-hand evidence that employment in your current workplace is not guaranteed, and you should not be complacent. So while you can breath a sigh of relief because your stream of income will not immediately cease, your respite may be short-lived. You still need to focus on your next move.

To avoid internalizing the disruption these decisions may cause, remember the decision was not yours and had nothing to do with you. The decision to lay someone off was likely made after much thought, analysis, and contemplation. In some cases, such business decisions are made after months, or even years, of long-term planning related to the future of a company. Not only have the majority of the laid-off people I have worked with been aware that a change in employment status was inevitable, but many were surprised that the job elimination or the termination did not occur months before it actually did.

So now that we have established that you have no ownership or responsibility for the decision, let's look at how you can turn the negative situation into a positive one.

On the most basic level, these terminations are a confirmation that your company is not immune from competitive and financial pressures. And, if any of the layoffs were performance-based, then this is a sign that your employer monitors job performance and reacts to it. Therefore, if your employer has spoken with you about your job performance or your attitude, or has made a suggestion that this company might not be the right fit, you should take this advice to heart because it seems like your employer may take action based on these concerns. These circumstances are all signs that you might be next in line. Rather than demoralize you, this situation should recharge you because it confirms that your primary job—finding a new job—is well worth the effort and should continue in full force.

Now, let's talk a bit about your coworker whose employment is coming to an end. People who are faced with the ending of an employment relationship, either by termination or layoff, often want to maintain a connection. Departing employees may not be eager to maintain a relationship with the decision-makers, but it is quite likely they will want to maintain contact with others who were removed from the decision. Think of this as a divorce. Friendships that provided support and comfort often become part of the division of assets. People going through a divorce welcome support from friends to temper the sense of isolation they believe may be forthcoming. The same is true for a departing employee who on Monday was surrounded by supportive colleagues and friends, but on Friday finds himself alone.

Under these circumstances, a supportive email, phone call, or invitation to lunch might be an incredibly welcome gesture. Someone who was just laid off is likely to be incredibly receptive to any effort or potential opportunity to continue work relationships. Perhaps it will be in a different form, such as a monthly phone call or dinner, but any type of stability will likely be welcome. Further, departing individuals will likely embrace some type of assurance that their connection to their former company, which may

> "When opportunity knocks, some people are in the backyard looking for four-leaf clovers."
>
> **POLISH PROVERB**

have been developing for a number of years, will not be eradicated overnight. Instead, the individual might see your gesture as a way to enable them to stay in touch with former colleagues, and stay informed as to how the industry is changing (or even on the latest workplace gossip).

This time of transition is the perfect opportunity to reach out to the individual to offer guidance and support. This is an ideal time to establish strong connections because people tend to bond and solidify close personal relationships in response to challenging circumstances. When faced with the news of the layoff of a colleague, that employee is likely to experience a range of emotions. They may be embarrassed, scared, frustrated, and unsure about their future livelihood. Explain that while it is easy for you to say, things will work out. Being laid off is no longer a rare occurrence, but instead a part of the working experience. Suggest this is an opportunity to be seized. Agree that it may take some time and it might not be an ideal situation, but inevitably it will work out. At some point a new job will be secured, income will be re-established, and in many cases, with the passage of time, the layoff will become viewed as a blessing in disguise.

As you speak to the departing employee, you may obtain some useful information that you can use as you try to maintain your employment until you secure a new opportunity. The departing employee may offer information that she obtained during her exit interview related to plans for her position and work, or she may know what other employees were impacted by the organization changes. Perhaps the employer revealed whether future rounds of layoffs are inevitable, and what other changes might be afoot. All of this information will be a valuable source of information for you. Jen Bellman, a 24-year-old computer specialist, credits just this kind of information gathering with saving her job.

> When computer specialist David Rangler, 55, was laid off, most of the department limited their interactions with him because he was not a particularly well-liked boss. In contrast, Jen Bellman wanted to support David and suggested that they have a drink after work.
>
> During that conversation, David warned Jen not to be forth-coming with any of her employment concerns during the company's newly introduced executive coaching sessions. Jen was familiar with those meetings and had recently been invited to attend an upcoming session. Past participants have discussed those "confidential" sessions as a productive way to "clear the air" and move past any personal workplace conflicts that had the potential to escalate. According to

David, however, the information he shared in those meetings was used as the basis for terminating his employment. In addition, he explained that, after he was fired he learned that Michael Deller, a paid consultant, attended those meetings not to review ways to improve the program (as had been announced), but to prepare reports summarizing the concerns aired in those meetings for the company's executive committee to review.

Solidifying bonds, particularly with a departing supervisor, can yield another significant benefit. In Jen's case, she can now use David as an employment reference, which can further her own career. This way, prospective employers can speak to someone familiar with her current employment position, without alerting her current boss of the fact that she's seeking alternative job opportunities outside of the company.

Although your core professional network consists of the people with whom you have worked, just as important are the secondary and tertiary connections: the colleagues of your colleagues, and the colleagues of the colleagues of your colleagues. Based on this framework, when someone you work alongside moves on to a new company, your network significantly grows as you expand your reach into new companies.

On the first day of any of the classes I teach, I ask my students if they know each other. They almost always say no. In response, I tell them that the interactive nature of my classes will not only enable them to get to know their fellow students, but will show them how getting to know other people is important to their professional careers. When they ask me to elaborate, I explain that if there are thirty-six people enrolled in a course, and each students has one internship and two different jobs over the next five years, by the end of the semester every student will have a potential connection to as many as 105 employers (35 X 3 = 105). This goes to show that it's not just who you know, but getting to know as many people as you can in the course of your working life.

People move from job to job throughout their careers. The larger and more transient your core group of colleagues is, the quicker your network grows and the quicker your reach expands. The departure of any one employee, regardless of the circumstances, branches your network out to a new department, new company, new industry, or new geographic location.

Whenever any of my former colleagues left for a new adventure (either involuntary or of their own accord), I'd always offer to provide assistance with any future employment matters. Not only was this offer genuine, but it allowed me to see how other employers managed their employees, and the types of employment agreements that were offered across the country. As a result, I have learned how various employers across the country handle the same employment issues.

As you speak with departing employees, it may be difficult to maintain your own morale. Your initial response might be to reduce your workplace effort, seeing it as an exertion of effort for which there is no reward. Or you may opt to "work to rule," meaning you perform just the tasks that need to be done to maintain your employment—nothing more, nothing less. You report to work at 9, leave at 5, take your full lunch, and decline to work after hours.

As tempting as that may be, however, do not stoop down to that level. Instead, as you work to solidify your relationship with the departing employee, be sure to devote time and energy to the workplace environment where you remain.

One of the primary purposes of a layoff is to reorganize the company in order to save money. If things are changing, there is nothing to prevent the implementation of a plan that changes your employment status for the better. The downside of reorganization is that jobs are eliminated. But the upside is that you may have access to different jobs—perhaps at higher levels with opportunities to obtain experience that spans more functions. If two functions are combined, this means that one person who previously performed one function might be asked to complete two (for probably more money). For example, a company might eliminate a director position that offers a salary of $150,000, and divide that work between the two remaining managers. This might include dual promotions to senior manager positions with a 25-percent increase to their $100,000 salaries. This would enable the company to save $100,000 in salary costs, plus all the other fringe and business costs associated with retaining a third employee. If you are working for a company that implements this strategy, you want to be sure that you are conducting yourself in a professional manner while these decisions are being made.

Further, even if the company declines to create a new position after a layoff, assuming that the departing employee worked forty hours a week, there are forty hours of weekly work that needs to be completed. Each task or interaction previously engaged in by someone other than you represents a tangible and immediate opportunity waiting to be seized.

By taking on more work (regardless of the specific parameters surrounding the new tasks), you're telling your employer that you are committed to your job, even under challenging circumstances. Not only that, you're increasing your value to the company, not to mention your job security as you continue to look for a new opportunity.

Further, few employees have an identical group of colleagues. Accepting new work will likely introduce you to a new group of people with whom you might not have previously interacted. These new people will become members of your professional network. And since your network will be an important component of your career success, just a few additions to your established group can result in a wealth of new information and opportunities for future success. Accepting some of the work previously performed by the departing employees could also enable you to learn about other opportunities that might exist in other parts of the company. Both the skills you develop and the people you meet may provide you with access to new job opportunities that you did not know existed prior to the individual's departure.

Lorraine Sandler, 51, felt trapped in her job as a director of human resources for a large manufacturing company where she had worked for eleven years. Lorraine felt pigeonholed in her position, while her requests for additional job responsibilities and career advancements were routinely declined.

Despite her discouragement, when Lorraine learned that the company decided to terminate the employment of a coworker who was involved in labor negotiations for the company, she reached out to the head of the department to offer assistance. The department head eagerly took advantage of Lorraine's knowledge of the company's benefit plans and provided her with a small role in the negotiation process. That additional experience enabled Lorraine to develop new skills and update her resume, which she eventually parlayed into a new position as an executive director of human resources and labor relations at another company, and at a substantial salary increase.

"SOMEONE ELSE GOT THE PROMOTION."

You do your job and you do it well. You are more than happy to do whatever project or menial tasks your boss asks you to do. You can even provide a list of times when you volunteered to take on additional work before anyone even asked. You get favorable feedback on a regular basis. According to your annual performance reviews, you continue to exceed your employer's expectations and add significant value to the company. Your boss regularly speaks of her appreciation for you and your work, and she agrees that it is time for you to advance. Yet you continue to be passed over for promotions at your company.

"Yesterday I was a dog. Today I'm a dog. Tomorrow I'll probably still be a dog. Sigh... There's so little hope for advancement.**"**

SNOOPY

CHARLES M. SCHULZ

Believe it or not, these turndowns are actually valuable sources of information. Not only that, they may be the perfect launching pads for other opportunities. That's because they provide you with a concrete road map about where you should direct your efforts.

The time and resources you dedicate to your job search are precious commodities. Use them as efficiently as possible. The more information you can gather—from whatever sources—the more effectively you can allocate your time and resources to situations that are most likely to yield significant results. Even more importantly, this feedback will enable you to stop wasting precious time and resources on opportunities that have little, if any, chance of success.

Albert Einstein defined insanity as doing the same thing over and over and expecting different results. You do not have time for insanity—you only have time to identify rewards and claim them.

If you have been denied a promotional opportunity, carefully assess the situation to learn from it and perhaps modify your job-seeking techniques. The way you use the information will vary, depending on whether you are passed over for a promotional opportunity for an internal candidate (someone else at your company) or an external candidate (someone who worked for a different company).

PASSED OVER FOR AN INTERNAL CANDIDATE

If you are passed over for an internal candidate, it should be fairly easy to gather some information about the person. Objectively compare and contrast yourself to the successful candidate. Is he or she aligned with some key decision-makers with whom you have had little (or even worse, negative) interactions? Is the newly hired candidate known for working late hours, while you are packing up your personal belongings to head home or to tend to other obligations? Does the successful candidate regularly make presentations at meetings? Do you see that person actively participating in brainstorming discussions at which you take a more passive approach?

This information will not only paint a picture of the type of candidate you should become, but it will increase your chances of receiving the job offer when other opportunities arise. If all of the promoted employees became friends with Sam the senior executive, stop by his office tomorrow and introduce yourself. If other promoted candidates tend to make themselves visible at "optional" meetings (such as holiday parties, informal workplace gatherings, and other events you'd rather avoid), guess what? Perhaps you ought to go to those things to make yourself visible, too. If Sally was promoted because she has an M.B.A. or a particular certification (and you weren't because you don't), you might want to look into night classes that can help you earn an advanced educational degree. Along the same lines, if the problem is with your current boss (in that no one who has worked under him has ever been promoted), you might consider a lateral transfer, either within the company or outside of it, to overcome that barrier.

Similarly, if you are a manager looking to advance to a director spot, and no one at your company has ever been promoted to a director position from anything other than a senior manager title, then you may need to adjust your short-term goals to make it more likely you will achieve long-term success.

Many companies approach career advancement opportunities with particular formulas in mind. The key to success is to figure out what the formula at your company is, and then devote your time and energy to ensuring you have all of the elements that will enable you to fit that formula.

PASSED OVER FOR AN EXTERNAL CANDIDATE

If you are passed over for a promotional opportunity in favor of an external candidate, your approach will be a bit different. First, is this a rare occurrence or standard company practice? In the event internal candidates are always passed over for promotional opportunities for external candidates, you need to redirect your efforts toward external opportunities, rather than any within the organization. I am always amazed at how many people tell me they continued to work for a company because they were told they were going to be promoted, when year after year they are passed over, making it obvious that the promotion will never materialize.

Many people tell me that they did not receive a promotion, raise, or significant bonus because the company did not have the money. Maybe that's true. But it's also possible that the company *does* have the money... but doesn't want to give it to you. Meaning, most employers will promote you, develop you, and go out of their way to keep you, so long as your continued employment continues to benefit them. But if you ask for advancement opportunities and are told they do not exist (or notice that they're bringing in external candidates to fill those positions), these are signs that your future with this employer is limited. You need to look elsewhere.

Assuming the hiring of an external candidate is an exception rather than the rule, you can use this situation to your advantage by befriending the external candidate. That will enable you to carry out the same analysis as if an internal candidate was hired. Once again, you want to find out what specific skills and experience you have in common with the individual who received the job offer, and which skills you lack. This is important because in some cases it might have made business sense for the company to look to an outsider.

Let's say your company is converting one of its current technological systems to a new system. It might be wise for them to recruit someone with vast experience in the new system to lead the project. If you learn there was some special circumstance that made an external candidate uniquely attractive, it probably makes sense to continue to pursue internal promotional opportunities.

If it turns out you share a similar background with the external candidate, but the outsider has training in certain areas that you lack, attempt to secure those qualifications. If possible, speak with the people who made the ultimate decision to hire the external candidate to get their read

on how you can increase the likelihood that you will be the best qualified candidate for the next promotional opportunity. If you are told the
external candidate brought skills to the job that you lacked, ask whether
the company will provide you with
assistance in obtaining that training.
This could simply be the opportunity
to shadow others in the company who
might possess those skills. Doing this

> "If plan A fails, remember
> there are 25 more letters."
> CHRIS GUILLEBEAU

would enable you to enhance your resume by developing a new skill and
also expand your network with the people you are shadowing. If the
company is unwilling to invest in your development, look for ways to
obtain those skills outside of regular business hours, then exploit your
new skills outside the company.

If an external candidate is hired for a position for which you applied and
for which you believe you were qualified, your top priority is to find out
about the job the new hire vacated. If you have similar qualifications to
the new hire, and if the newly hired person gave her former employer the
customary two weeks' notice, there may be a newly vacated job for which
you are qualified right under your nose. You should be able to get some
broad information about the vacated position by reviewing any new hire
announcement or introduction made at company meetings, on company
websites, or in company newsletters.

Although adopting these strategies may seem time-consuming, once you
put them into place they will simply become part of your daily routine.
Remember, lining up your next job is your most important job. If you
want to guarantee yourself a continued stream of income for life, you
need to accept that you will always be spending time looking for potential
opportunities and ways to ensure you are qualified for them.

Just as when people around you are terminated or laid off, when a new
person is brought into a position you can use that to your advantage. A
new hire is going to need someone to show her the ropes and educate
her about how things work. Rather than being resentful (particularly if

she got the job or promotion that you wanted for yourself), see this as a chance to establish a strong connection with someone who is desperate for allies. If the new hire can in any way influence your terms and conditions of employment, you can bet they'll remember your kindness.

> When the vice-president position at a large insurance company became available, a number of seemingly qualified internal candidates applied for the position. They were all passed over for an external candidate, Andrew Sellers, 44, who had a personal connection with a number of senior executives at the company. With the exception of Phil Edwards, 55, the existing team resented Andrew and collectively decided they would do nothing to contribute to his success. As it happens, Andrew was laid off just eight months later, when the company decided to move in a new direction.

> A few years later, Phil found himself out of work as a result of a company merger. While Phil struggled to find work, Andrew had landed a coveted position in a new company. When Phil reached out to him, Andrew was happy to create a long-term temporary position for Phil as he looked for (and eventually found) another permanent position.

To this day, Andrew feels indebted to Phil for his success and helping him to last as long as he did at the original insurance company. Phil feels indebted to Andrew for assisting him in securing his current position because the temporary position enabled him to avoid the stigma of unemployment (and provided him a stream of income) as he applied for new permanent opportunities.

"EVERYONE IS GETTING BETTER JOBS ELSEWHERE AND I'M STUCK."

You are unhappy in your current job and have been expending significant efforts on your job search, and yet it seems like everyone is able to land better opportunities except for you. First, when you hear about how great other peoples' new jobs are, keep in mind that the grass is often greener on the other side because it is fertilized with bullshit. It is unlikely that their situations are as fantastic as they suggest. Besides, as people leave, you are presented with further opportunities to thrive. Put differently, don't compare your insides to other people's outsides. Everyone is likely facing the same challenges as you, but you will likely never know the exact circumstances surrounding their situations.

Life coach, columnist, and best-selling author Martha Beck often writes about "FOMO," an acronym for the fear of missing out. This concept, Beck says, refers to the unsettling feelings we have when reviewing Facebook and other social media websites, only to see that everyone other than ourselves seems to be living life to the fullest, particularly when compared to our lives that feel fraught with difficulties.

When reviewing the social media postings authored by hundreds of our closest and perhaps not-so-close friends, it appears that everyone is out to dinner at the finest restaurants, cooking the most fabulous meals, and consistently surrounded by their perfect families and crowds of friends. This consistent receipt of positive information about others, Beck says, results in people feeling depressed and inadequate because their lives do not compare to the inaccurate representations of the lives of others.

> **"**The grass is often greener on the other side because it is fertilized with bullshit.**"**
>
> **UNKNOWN**

Beck points out that when your Facebook-obsessed friend pulls out a camera at dinner and directs everyone to say "cheese," the shared realization that the picture will end up on Facebook within minutes forces everyone to grin ear to ear regardless of how bored they are with the same stories, how exhausted they are, how terrible the meal was, and how many other places they would rather be.

I have a friend who starts each of our conversations telling me how great her job is. When the economy tanked and everyone was concerned about losing their job, she told me things were great, that she did the work of four people and was highly valued and well compensated, and that she believed there was no way she would ever be let go. Though I never begrudged her success, I always envied the excitement she felt about day-to-day life.

One evening we walked home together from a regularly scheduled bi-monthly dinner with a few friends. The dinner and conversation were pleasant, but nothing out of the ordinary. On our walk we bumped into a former coworker and stopped for a brief chat. My friend proceeded to explain that we were coming from an incredible evening at a new trendy venue, where we caught up with a large group of our jet-setting friends. I wondered if we had been at the same dinner.

That experience taught me to put people's claims in perspective, and to focus on my needs instead of comparing my status to others. This is a lesson Evan wishes he had learned earlier.

Evan Lively is a 32-year-old single man from Boston. After graduating from a prestigious law school, Evan accepted a job at a top law firm, knowing he would be able to earn a significant amount of money to pay down the six-figure loan he had taken to fund his education. Evan knew the sacrifice this would entail: working seven days a week, sometimes up to eighteen hours a day, and likely having to forgo many personal commitments during his first couple of years at the firm. However, Evan felt that these sacrifices would be short-lived and the job would provide him with security, a highly competitive salary, and a spot on the coveted partnership track of the firm that would ensure a lifetime of benefits.

Evan quickly learned the job required even more sacrifice than he had anticipated. After working until 5am and then returning at 10am after a brief nap and change of clothes, he was questioned about his late arrival. Regardless of how quickly he worked, there were always new assignments piling up, and aggressive deadlines to be met. When taking an overnight flight for a rare weekend retreat, he was specifically instructed to set up his out-of-office assistant on his email to say he was sorry for the inconvenience and would be unavailable for a few hours during the middle of the night. When attending a play on a Saturday evening, he had to leave during the intermission to complete the review of a file that had to be returned between the second and third acts. Evan learned that his hard work and sacrifices were nothing to be applauded, but rather fair exchange for the compensation he received.

Evan kept telling himself the sacrifice was worth it until he found himself excluded from meetings where new projects were discussed. Then he was disinvited to other meetings because, he was told, he had so much other work to do. This was in spite of the fact that many other attorneys in the firm with similar workloads were asked to attend these gatherings. In addition, he started receiving unfair criticism, unrealistic expectations, and continued isolation. Finally, when the firm was about to welcome its class of incoming junior associates, Evan was told that since he "could not possibly maintain that pace much longer," he should look for work elsewhere. He was told he could continue to report to work for the next three months while he searched for other jobs. Evan felt betrayed, rejected, and angry. He also felt angry with himself for being naïve.

Evan soon regrouped emotionally and started searching for a new position. He had a three-month deadline to avoid having to explain why he would leave a coveted six-figure job without another job lined up. With no savings he could not afford to forgo his income for even a short period of time.

Six days prior to the official end of his employment, Evan secured a position as an in-house attorney. When word spread about his new job, many of Evan's soon-to-be former peers reached out to ask how they could follow in his footsteps. He decided not to divulge the details of what had transpired during the prior six months. Instead he talked about the positive experience he had with the firm and its commitment to his success. Evan did not want to risk the firm leaking that he had actually been let go.

After a few months at her new job, Evan felt comfortable sharing his experience with others. He was stunned to learn that what happened to him was not unique and, in some industries, is a common practice. Employers know that their recruitment efforts will suffer in the event they garner a reputation for terminating employees, so "stealth firings" enable them to keep their reputation intact while ending relationships with those they feel do not add value to the company.

> "I have not failed. I've just found 10,000 ways that won't work."
>
> **THOMAS A. EDISON**

The moral of the story? There's no place for Pollyannas in the loyalty-free workplace. No job is quite as wonderful as it may seem or as you have been told.

"I KEEP GETTING REJECTED AT THE LATER STAGES OF THE INTERVIEW PROCESS."

You are eager to advance your career, you exert significant time and effort to the process, you continue to interview for different opportunities (sometimes returning to the same employer on multiple occasions), but you have not gotten an offer. Of course this is discouraging. You may feel like there is no use in continuing on this path, since it has produced no results. Do not give up!

When professional athletes are in a slump, they do not go home and hide under the covers for the next week. Instead, they continue to practice—perhaps doubling their efforts—so they can learn from their mistakes and be prepared for the next game or event and all those that follow. The real value to failing is that it gets you a step closer to identifying and emulating what works, and identifying and stopping what does not.

The good news is that, while the results may indicate otherwise, you're do-ing some things right. After all, you can't land a job without an interview, and you landed an interview. Employers receive hundreds of resumes for every vacancy. For every job seeker who's invited to come in for an inter-view, there are countless others who never get past the initial screening process, never receive face-to-face interaction with the decision-makers, or never even get an acknowledgment that their application was consid-ered. The fact that you not only received a response, but were invited to participate in the interview process shows, at a minimum, that there was something about your application and your credentials that made you a viable candidate. That puts you significantly ahead of your competition.

On top of that, even an unsuccessful interview provides a new avenue to pursue.

Think of the interview process as a personal focus group. You now have a chance to get feedback regarding what skills you need to develop to become more marketable. And, this feedback will come from people who have direct and firsthand knowledge about your qualifications. Each and every person you spoke with, met with, or came in contact with, rep-resents a new source of targeted information. Reach out and get some concrete and specific guidance as to what you need to do to change future results. You have a perfect opportunity to find out what went wrong and make it right.

> "Be thankful for the bad things in life. For they opened your eyes to good things you weren't paying attention to before."
>
> **KERMIT THE FROG**

The people you reach out to will vary, depending on whom you spoke with during the process and how the process unfolded. Maybe you worked with an in-house recruiter who made the initial contact and was your guide throughout the process. If so, she should be your first source of feedback. Thank the recruiter for her time and efforts, and express your disappointment in not having been selected as the finalist for the posi-tion. Then arrange a time to speak with her further.

This may be a difficult conversation to have, but it's critical. Remember the decision made was a business one, not a personal one. As much as you are hurt, discouraged, or angered by the decision, those feelings will quickly dissipate if the recruiter calls you a few months from now with another opportunity for which you are better qualified.

When speaking with the recruiter, there are three things you want to know:

1. Why you didn't get the job.
2. Who got the job.
3. Whether there might be other jobs at the company for which you are qualified.

You want to find out about any concerns the final decision-makers had about your candidacy and see if you can modify your behavior to address them in the future. I have had some clients who were informed that their qualifications were a fit for the position, but their interview style was too lax—or that their aggressive responses to some of the questions suggested overconfidence, which in turn suggested that they would be unreceptive to constructive criticism.

Even if you disagree with it, such feedback can help you with future interviews because it tells you how others perceive you. If, for example, prospective employers provide you with similar feedback (or feedback that centers on the same common themes), this information can and should inform your future conversations.

When you speak with the recruiters, you will also want to learn whether there were any substantive concerns the decision-makers had with your candidacy. If the recruiter informs you that you were qualified, but felt your skills in a particular area were underdeveloped (or strong in certain areas but weak in others), now you know what steps to take in the future. Similarly, if something about your resume was the problem, you might want to rewrite or even eliminate that information from future applications.

Julie Sloven, 23, had a number of internships with labor unions while in college. After graduating from a small liberal arts university, she decided she wanted to pursue a career representing management. Julie highlighted her union-side experience on her resume, believing it would be viewed as an indication of her commitment to working in the field. After a few interviews and feedback from decision-makers, Julie realized that the way she communicated her experience concerned some potential employers. They inferred that her primary goal was to continue to work for a labor union, but that she had not been able to get that kind of job. Prospective employers did view her experience as indicative of a commitment to the field, which is why she received so many interview invitations in the first place. But they also saw her past experience as an indication of her commitment to representing certain interests, that were not necessarily aligned with their own.

To remedy this perception Julie did some pro bono work representing employers. She also wrote a few articles about how her past experiences representing employees steered her towards a new direction to want to represent employers. She then referenced those publications on her resume. Julie also revised her cover letter and resume to reflect a more balanced approach.

In addition, because she was aware of these concerns, Julie kept them in her mind as she interviewed for future positions. She made it a point to tailor each of her responses to emphasize her management-side work. Any time she spoke about her union-side work, she made sure to explain how it would add value to her future role as an employer advocate.

When speaking with the recruiters about why you did not get an offer, you will likely get some information about the candidate who was selected. This information will enable you to compare and contrast your skills and qualifications with that of the person who received the offer. This can guide you as you devise next steps in your process. Perhaps the hired candidate had specific experience you were lacking, or the successful candidate had experience similar to you but presented it in a different way. Maybe the hired candidate had previous dealings with the company or decision-makers, indicating that if you intend to apply for future positions with the same company, you should develop those types of relationships. If the person who was offered the position was hired internally, perhaps you might need to redirect your efforts to secure a more junior position so you are in the pipeline for higher-level positions in the future.

By finding out about the candidate who is going to fill the new position, you'll also learn about the position that person vacated. If the candidate hired had a bit more experience than you, it is possible you are a viable candidate for their prior position. If their prior position was

> **"I've learned that something constructive comes from every defeat."**
>
> **TOM LANDRY**

seen as a necessary prerequisite for jobs at the level for which you are applying, working in that vacancy might be the ideal way to fill a gap in your candidacy.

In some instances, a recruiter will reveal where the other person came from, within the context of trying to explain to you why you did not receive the offer. In the event the recruiter is not forthcoming with information about the new candidate, at a minimum you will be provided with some clues as to their identity.

Advertising executive Tim Brewers, 36, interviewed for a director level position at a large cosmetics company. After the third round of interviews, the hiring manager called to inform him that although he was a strong contender for the position, the company decided to extend an offer to another candidate who had been working in a comparable role at the company's key competitor. Because Tim had done extensive research in preparation for his interviews, he knew which companies they identified as their key competitors. With some quick research and deductive reasoning, Tim was able to identify the successful candidate and submit his resume for the vacated position.

Even if the recruiter does not provide enough information to figure out the successful candidate's identity, you can often find this information through other avenues. If the position is fairly senior, review the company's website to see if an announcement is made about the new hire. Such announcements often prominently list the candidate's prior experience. Similarly, if you are following the company with whom you interviewed on a networking website like LinkedIn, you may very well see an update of its profile announcing new additions to their staff.

Herbert Blackhorn, 48, held a Ph.D. and worked as an academic administrator for his entire career. Eager to take his career to the next level, Herbert spent more than six months interviewing to be a member of the senior cabinet of the president of a large academic institution. The process included a screening interview, a number of interviews with key leaders, an interview with the entire hiring committee, and a full day at the academic institution shadowing other members of the senior team. After a lengthy and exhaustive process, Herbert was passed over for the opportunity.

Although the recruiter for that position was not interested in providing him with any feedback as to why he was not selected, a lengthy announcement about the new hire, including the position she vacated, appeared on the institution's website soon after the decision was made. Since Herbert knew a number of people who worked for the institution from where the new hire came, he was able to use those connections to get more insight into the departing employees' prior experience. This information provided Herbert with some new ideas about how he could develop his skills and enhance his resume to make him more qualified for other similar opportunities that might arise in the future.

If the person hired was an internal candidate, ask the recruiter about the hiring plan for the position that the promoted employee will be vacating. Although recruiters often welcome the promotion of internal candidates, some find internal transfers frustrating because even after a successful placement, the number of vacancies remains the same. Therefore, a recruiter may be incredibly receptive to your willingness to be considered for a more junior role, since you have already been partially vetted through the process. Even if you are not a viable match, this sends a message that you remain interested in working for the company and will consider all potential suitable opportunities.

Remember, one of the primary job responsibilities of recruiters is to network. They regularly exchange information about open positions and available talent with other recruiters, companies, and individuals. It is likely they will welcome the opportunity to remain connected to you. Aside from the benefit the recruiter can derive from remaining connected to you personally, they will also see you as a connection to everyone else in your network.

Recruiters belong to private email groups that target specific industries, geographic locations, employers, and even job titles. They exchange information about particular candidates, whether positive or negative, as a means of helping one another find the most suitable matches for their vacancies. Quite often they are happy to refer the candidate to other departments at the company, or even to other companies, in the hope that the favor will be returned.

David Waters, 41, applied for a position as a pharmacist at a large retail chain in Philadelphia. In a post-interview conversation with the human resources director, he learned he was passed over in favor of a pharmacist who had previously done temporary work for the company.

David immediately reached out to the director to thank her. The recruiter said she was so impressed with David's qualifications, as well as the fact he took the time to inquire as

to how he could gain entry into the company, that she recommended David for a comparable position with one of the
company's subsidiaries. He landed that job and still holds it.

If you interview for a position that is brought to you by an independent
or external recruiter (as opposed to one employed by the company con-
ducting the job search), you'll want to have this same conversation. It is
likely the recruiter will initiate this dialogue, especially if you got far in
the process and the recruiter is confident that you'll receive some kind
of offer in the future. It is in an independent recruiter's best interest to
identify your strengths and weaknesses so that they can prepare you for
future opportunities that may materialize.

Independent recruiters receive a fee for placing a candidate in a position.
If you don't get placed in a job, they don't get paid. Therefore, it is in the
recruiter's interest to work with you to eliminate any potential barriers
to your success. Of course, if your interview is a complete disaster, or the
recruiter becomes aware of a significant issue concerning your performance, they may sever ties (which, assuming you're already aware of the
mishap, should come as no surprise).

After speaking to the in-house or external recruiter, try to get some
feedback from the actual people who interviewed you (either through the
interviewers themselves, or by way of the recruiter). Most hiring decisions are the result of discussions and exchanges of information between
different people. Many people were consulted about your candidacy.
Any comments you can access, from whatever the source, can prove valuable. Comments made at the time of the interview will provide insight
into the first impression you make. Comments about your professional
expertise can provide guidance about how you can better inform other
prospective employers about your qualifications, or what areas you need
to develop to increase your likelihood of success.

I recall speaking with 31-year-old Wendy Saunders, who showed up to a
day of interviews, only to realize that the first interviewer was the father
of a long-term ex-boyfriend. The passage of six years since the end of

the relationship and the coloring and straightening of Wendy's curly brown hair made her unrecognizable to him, though she immediately recognized him. When I asked whether this was awkward, she said that since she had a great relationship with her ex-boyfriend's family (and with her ex-boyfriend's father in particular), the conversation was actually pleasant. To my surprise, however, the conversations with the subsequent interviewers challenged Wendy the most. When I asked how the others would even know of this coincidence, Wendy told me that after a few introductory remarks with the second interviewer, ("So how do you feel your missed-opportunity-of-a-father-in-law has aged" was one of the questions), she knew that each interviewer passed comments about their conversation to the interviewer that followed.

The point is, everyone talks with one another to discuss information gathered during the interview process. This can be a wonderful benefit if you present well during an interview, but problematic if you do not. This makes it critical that you solicit feedback after an interview that does not lead to a job offer, so that you are able to identify anything that may prevent you from getting an offer.

Blair Davenport, 26, went in for the third and presumably final round of interviews for a job as an administrative coordinator in a healthcare facility. Blair not only told me the interviews went exactly as planned, but joked that during the interview she focused on where to put her prized cactus in her soon-to-be office. Imagine her shock when she learned that the offer went to someone else. She could not fathom what went wrong.

I convinced Blair to reach out to the human resources director, with whom she established a strong connection throughout the process. In fact, it was she who told Blair prior to the interview that the job "was hers to lose." Needless to say, the human resources director was just as embarrassed by the outcome. However, when she spoke to the executives, they told her that Blair came across as arrogant and presumptuous. (As it happens, Blair actually *did* joke about where she would place her prized cactus.) Even though the executives were ready to extend her an offer, they felt her attitude would not fit well with the laid-back culture of the company.

Ironically, Blair is actually quite humble. Yet she was under the impression that the last round of interviews was merely a formality. The upshot? The human resources director assured Blair that she would not hesitate to recommend her for future opportunities, while Blair now approaches all interviews with much more formality to avoid a repeat of this situation.

Another reason why you can benefit from a rejection: Regardless of the outcome, your participation in the interview can become a valuable networking tool.

Let's say that prior to this interview process you had no connection to the company. That meant there was nothing to separate you from the hundreds of others applying to work there. Now you have established a personal connection with the in-house recruiter, someone in human resources,

> "Experience is what you get when you don't get what you want."
>
> **TORI FILLER**

and perhaps a few others. The next time an opportunity materializes, you should still apply in the manner requested in the job announcement—but you can also forward your application to those with whom you have a prior relationship. That way, you can make sure your information gets into the hands of the right people.

In addition, the people who interviewed you likely have other professional contacts that work in similar roles. If you interview with Jim from the IT department for a position and do not receive an offer, if Jim likes your experience, he may let you know about a similar opening at his friend's company. Every time you connect with someone, you increase the chances of learning of an opportunity that exists within their network.

Jack Edmonton, 44, had a number of interviews with a large bank, only to be passed over for an internal candidate. Jack refused to be discouraged and continued looking for a new job. Six months later, Jack interviewed for and accepted an offer for a comparable position at a different banking institution. A few weeks after starting in his new role, Jack met the bank's outside counsel. The attorney told Jack he should treat him well because he was responsible for the bank's offer of employment.

The outside counsel explained that he was also outside counsel for the other bank where Jack had interviewed months before. The outside counsel had worked closely with the other bank, and the bank's internal recruiter had confided in him that its hiring decision was a difficult choice because they had a strong second choice for that role. So, when another bank asked the outside counsel for a recommendation for its vacancy, he mentioned Jack's name and noted that he was a strong second choice for the prior role with a competing bank. When the recruiter found his cover letter and resume in the stack of applications he received for this position, he pulled it from the pile and started the interview process, knowing a competitor thought highly of Jack's qualifications.

Maintaining a connection with people with whom you interviewed can result in other indirect benefits. I interviewed a number of times with a large media company that has the reputation for being difficult to penetrate. The company is a stellar employer, and the limited turnover makes it even harder for an outsider to break in. Although my qualifications were never a perfect match for any of the positions that I was called in to discuss, I was more than happy to meet with the recruiter any time she reached out to me.

A few months ago, a client told me she had not received a response to an application she submitted to this company. I told my client about my relationship with the recruiter, and suggested she send me the cover letter and resume she had previously submitted online. I passed the material on to the recruiter, along with a brief reminder of our past interactions and a glowing endorsement of my client. Within eighteen minutes of my client mentioning her interest to me, she was scheduled for a screening interview for the following day. I had also reinvigorated my relationship with a recruiter who appreciated the referral of a strong candidate.

As you move through your career, remember you will not build a meaningful network if you reach out to people only when you need something from them. You never know where the next opportunity will come from.

> Kaylee Singer, 24, works in catering and had been looking for a new job for over a year. Four months earlier she had told me she was scheduled for the fourth and final round of interviews for a job that would be significant job advancement. Because of this, I was quite surprised when Kaylee called to ask whether I had any connections to a laundry list of Fortune 500 companies where she had applied for a new job. I asked Kaylee what happened to the offer that she thought was a sure thing. She said the company was rude and merely sent her a generic form letter saying that her credentials were not a match for the vacancy. When I asked what they said when she followed up, Kaylee was silent— she said it never occurred to her to reach out for feedback.
>
> Here she was, reaching out to me for any indirect or tenuous connection to a list of her target employers. Yet she didn't seek advice or guidance from the recruiter with whom she'd established a personal connection (and who'd thought highly enough of her to grant her a job interview), or any of the other key decision-makers with whom she spent time and interacted.

Ben Franklin famously limited life's certainties to death and taxes. If he were around today, however, I'll bet he'd add one more: "In a loyalty-free workplace, the terms and conditions of employment will certainly change over the span of your working life."

You may have little or no control over this lack of stability, but you can control how you react to those changing circumstances so that you take advantage of the new opportunities that each situation creates.

Rejections are just a way for you to expand the size and reach of your network. As we'll see in the following chapter, your network is the springboard for unprecedented opportunities. Therefore, any opportunity to expand your network will increase the likelihood of you achieving those unprecedented results.

SECRET # 4

EXPAND YOUR HUNTING GROUNDS

By now you know that to secure a perpetual paycheck in the loyalty-free workplace, you have to revamp your approach to the job search process. For one thing, there are fewer jobs and more people applying for them. The economic downturn, technological advancements, the outsourcing of jobs, families that need two incomes instead of one, and the number of aging employees who are delaying retirement are among the many reasons. Company layoffs due to restructuring and mergers to increase efficiency and save money, not to mention the increase in terminations due to the refusal of employers to retain average performers in the loyalty-free workplace are also important factors.

Because of these circumstances, when speaking with members of your network, remember that you're competing for their shrinking resources. As much as someone in your network may want to help you, there are probably three others hoping to take advantage of the same leads.

The good news is that you can easily adapt to this new reality. All you need to do is expand your hunting grounds. By that I mean opening your eyes to a new way of looking at the much-maligned practice of networking.

Consider this. For most people, taking a shower, brushing our teeth, making our bed, and brushing our hair are part of our daily routines. We may see these things as chores, something we *have* to do, versus wanting to do. Granted, depending on one's circumstances, one can argue that we can all live a perfectly good life without doing any of these things. The flip side, of course, is that without exercise or dental hygiene, our health may suffer. This can materialize as heart disease, gum disease, and other complications that can impact our quality of life.

The same goes for networking. If you are truly committed to earning a perpetual paycheck, you have to network. There's no way around it. Yet you'd be amazed at the sheer number of job seekers today who are either lousy at networking, or choose not to network at all.

I often talk to people about the status of their job search process. Many find it depressing because of the amount of time they spend setting up and attending meet-

> "If you're not networking, you're not working."
> DENIS WAITLET

ings that produce no results. Because networking is a numbers game (or so they've been told), they engage in the same process over and over and over again:

Set up three meetings. *Check.*
Have those meetings. *Check.*
Get the names of three other people to meet. *Check.*
Set up *those* meetings. *Check.*
Those meetings produce more names. *Check.*

In other words, they repeat the same process, without getting anywhere. (Or, as I like to put it: Lather. Rinse. Repeat.) No wonder they feel depressed.

A young mother requires her husband to purchase an aluminum baking pan each Thanksgiving so that she can fold it slightly before placing it with the turkey into her oven, cooking the turkey in what becomes somewhat of a V-shaped pan. The woman does this year after year, in the presence of her daughters, who eventually ask why she folds the tray in that manner. "Because that's how Grandma did it," she replies.

One Thanksgiving, the still-curious children ask their grandmother why she folded the pan in the oven. To their surprise, the grandmother was surprised to hear that her daughter was still cooking the turkey that way. "When I raised your mother," she told her granddaughters, "we lived in a house that had only a small oven. The only way a roasting pan would fit was to collapse it in that manner."

Techniques that may have worked before may be obsolete today because circumstances change. Networking today is a brand-new game—but it's one that you can win, if you have the right tools and know how to play. The key is implementing a few simple and non-threatening strategies.

DON'T TALK TO STRANGERS

From an early age we are taught not to talk to strangers. For that reason, by the time we're adults many of us tend to avoid engaging strangers in conversation, even for just five minutes. This mindset likely infiltrates a number of components of our daily lives. We may first reach out to a babysitter we have known for years before we try out a new babysitter, even if the prospective new hire comes highly recommended. We may drive a bit out of our way to a gift store where we know the salesperson, even if we know there is another similar store in town. The fact is, it's human nature to gravitate to people we know and to help those who help us. This is precisely what happens in the workplace.

An employer calls one of its top employees into the office and says, "Son, you have worked for this company almost a full year. You started off in the mailroom, two weeks later you were moved to a sales position, and one month after that you were promoted to the coveted district manager position. Just two short months after, you became the vice-president, and now I am ready to announce my retirement and I want you to run the company. What do you think about that?

"Thank you," says the employee.

"Thanks? Is that all you have to say to me?"

"Oh, right, sorry. Thanks, Dad."

—UNKNOWN

You work alongside your colleagues eight hours a day, five days a week. Why would you want to lock yourself into this together-time with a complete stranger? Knowing how important our income is, if given the choice, why would anyone willingly give a complete stranger any opportunity to negatively impact their livelihood? The answer is simple: You wouldn't.

Here's the good news: When it comes to our relationships with our coworkers—or anyone else we meet on a regular basis—the difference between being labeled a stranger and a non-stranger is so minimal, even a small connection can bridge this gap.

When I was a young girl, and first started seeing my doctor for my annual physical, I always marveled at how comfortable she made me feel, almost always remembering some personal fact about me. "How's your new baby sister?" she asked when I was thirteen and my third sister was born. "Are you still working at the toy store?" she asked when I reached high school. "Did you take any more overnight road trips?" she asked one year, when even I barely recalled the trip she was talking about. Not only was my doctor incredibly personable, but by bringing up these seemingly minor details at the beginning of my visits, she immediately put me at ease. I felt like we were truly connected and that she really cared about me.

Let's fast forward to the time I saw her when I was twenty-two years old. After taking my vitals, the nurse accidentally left my chart in the examining room. (Ordinarily she'd leave it in the drop box located right outside the door). Being curious, I took a look at my chart. To my surprise, there was a bright sheet of paper listing many of the details my doctor had spoken of in the years before (new sister born, new job at a toy store, overnight road trip, college applications, wants to go to law school, etc.).

At first, I thought I'd been bamboozled—I thought my doctor had a really great memory and that she genuinely cared about me. Then I realized that those notes were just her way of establishing a connection with me. Not only that, it wasn't long before I started emulating this practice myself.

Once, at an event, I met a colleague who told me that she was slightly depressed because her oldest daughter was getting ready to leave for college. As it happened, her daughter was going to the same school from which I graduated. So, you can bet that the next time I saw this woman, I asked how her daughter was and whether she'd managed to secure housing in one of the better-known dorms. At the same event I met another woman who said she took advantage of any New York conference made available to her, solely because her daughter just started college in New York. You guessed it—the next time I ran into that newly minted member of my network, I asked her how her daughter was adjusting to life in the Big Apple.

The point is, people want to build relationships with one another. That's human nature. The best way to connect with people is by showing interest in someone else's life, no matter how tenuous that connection may seem.

This is precisely why networking is so important. Since we are told never to talk to strangers, it makes perfect sense that we resist bringing strangers into our workplaces. People want to work with people with whom they have a bond and know something about. This is why from the moment you first apply for a job, anything you can do to forge a connection with the other person will provide you with a significant advantage.

INFORMATIONAL INTERVIEWS ARE NO LONGER NECESSARY

We all know what an informational interview is, right? That's where you set up a meeting with a working professional to discuss the path that led them to their current position, as well as the pros and cons of their job. Then, at the end of the interview, you ask the working professional whether they know of any available positions (or, if not, the names and contact information of two or three other people who might know of a vacancy). It's not a job interview, per se, but rather a fishing expedition.

> Philip Hatch, 41, is the executive vice-president at a major news company in New York City. Philip recounts the stories of his fairly regular meetings with nervous but persistent job seekers who convince him to set up an informational meeting to discuss how he landed in his current position. At each of these meetings Philip finds himself sitting across from someone who stares at him in silence, wondering when the conversation will start. When Philip gently prompts the person across the table (at a lunch he will likely pay for) to explain the reason for the meeting, a blank stare is usually followed by an inquiry as to whether Phillip is aware of any jobs at the company he works for (or any other company that might give the job seeker a chance). When Philip responds, candidly and truthfully, that he is unaware of any current vacancies but will keep the candidate in mind, this is usually followed by a request from the job seeker for the contact information of any of Philip's friends who might know of any other jobs that might be a fit.

Like we said, informational interviews are like washing our hair, only without getting shiny hair in return. Rarely, if ever, does anything productive come out of such meetings. Yet job seekers continue to set them up because they believe that this is the best way to land their new job. We simply have to stop doing the same thing over and over just because we think it is how it is supposed to work. The evidence is in, this strategy is outdated, and we need to adapt. Lather. Rinse. Repeat. It works only in the shower.

What is pushing these traditional informational interviews further toward extinction is the fact that in today's economy there are more and more people competing for fewer and fewer jobs. Consequently, that also means there are more and more people requesting informational interviews, in the hopes of securing job leads. Not only that, but because people in the loyalty-free workplace are unemployed for longer periods of time than ever before, those who request informational meetings today do so for longer periods of time. Plus, there's the job turnover rate. In the loyalty-free workplace, people change jobs more often than they did before (usually after three to five years). That, of course, means even more competition. And since job seekers today are aware of the increased competition for informational interviews, they request even more informational interviews from a greater number of people to increase their chances of success. In other words, it's a perfect storm.

> "There is nothing so useless as doing efficiently that which should not be done at all."
>
> **PETER DRUCKER**

Given the fierce competition for jobs, you don't have time for meetings that will likely waste your time, or anyone else's. You need to have a very specific targeted plan to find your next job.

Now, before you get too excited, let's make one thing clear. Even in the loyalty-free workplace, you'll still have to schedule meetings, and you'll still need to talk to working professionals about their job experiences. You just have to approach it in a way that results in mutual benefits for you and the people you meet.

DOES THIS SOUND FAMILIAR?

If you are being truly honest, if you request an informational meeting with someone like Philip and tell them you're interested in their career path, what you really want to know is whether they know of any current opportunities. And, if not, you want to know whether they know of anyone who knows of vacancies. In today's workplace, however, this method is about as useful as folding an aluminum pan to cook a turkey.

First, when you reach out to someone to request a meeting, it is likely via email and you likely include some basic information about what you are looking for and attach a resume. Because of technological advancements related to how we request these meetings, within a short period of time after reading your email (perhaps even one or two minutes), the person you're querying will know whether they are aware of a potential opportunity that matches your qualifications. *If they're willing to share that information, they'll tell you—immediately.* This is in contrast to years ago, when these meetings were set up through administrative assistants. In most instances, the person with whom you were meeting knew next to nothing about you, or why they even had an appointment with you, until the meeting actually took place.

Given today's fast-paced world, if someone really wants to help you, an immediate response is the only response that makes sense. In the loyalty-free workplace, people move from job to job at a rapid pace, and exchange information just as quickly. It often takes time, perhaps up to a few weeks, for people to coordinate their schedules and schedule a meeting. If someone is aware of a job vacancy and waits until the meeting to share that information with you, by that time the job would likely no longer be vacant—or, if it remained unfilled, it is very likely the hiring process would be well underway.

Because of this dynamic, it no longer makes sense for these once obligatory meetings to play such a prominent role in your job search process. This is because once you have received the information you were requesting (i.e., you were told there is no job), there really is no need to have this meeting, because you have already gathered the information you sought. In addition, there is another significant reason why it makes sense to bypass this process.

EFFICIENT AND TARGETED ACCESS

In the past, if you wanted to meet with a senior executive at a particular company, but had a personal connection only with a middle manager, you might request a meeting with the middle manager with the hope that she might provide you with the contact information of the senior executive, if not introduce you directly. Today, thanks to email, referrals can be made with a lot less effort. This expanded access is positive because it has the potential to connect you more efficiently with the people you want to meet.

These technological advancements do, however, present new challenges because the fact that job seekers can streamline the process and schedule more meetings, even with the appropriate people, has drastically reduced the value of the meetings that do take place.

THE FLIP SIDE OF DIRECT ACCESS

In today's workplace, a simple email from someone in your network, or even a request to connect on LinkedIn has the potential to connect the job seeker directly with not only people who are currently working in their industry, but also the people in those people's networks.

> Bank CEO Mallory Wright, 52, emails her long-term friend and talent agent Vincent Ratner, 49, requesting that he schedule an informational meeting with the son of her client, an aspiring actor. Mallory copies the actor on this email request. Within minutes Vincent replies to the aspiring actor, suggesting that he come to his office the following Monday for a meeting.

The problem in this situation is that had Mallory waited until she saw Vincent at a social gathering, or perhaps called him to see whether he thought this meeting might be appropriate, Vincent could have told her that, because of protocol, he cannot provide any meaningful assistance to the aspiring actor. But because of how Mallory made the request (direct email to Vincent, with a CC to the actor), Vincent felt obligated to honor the request, even though the likelihood is that Mallory would receive little, if any, benefit from having attending it. So, the good news is that a meeting was arranged. The bad news is that the meeting is unlikely to produce a benefit.

Another problem with direct access is because it takes little effort to email a request for a meeting, job seekers tend to send the same pitch to as many companies as possible, rather than tailor it to each recipient. (This is also known as "spraying and praying," a concept we'll return to later.) In addition, assuming you do get a reply (and succeed in setting up a meeting), you're not as likely to spend as much time with the executive as you may have before. Whereas once upon a time working professionals might have devoted as much as two hours providing guidance to an eager job seeker, because of the sheer number of requests they receive today, you might get fifteen minutes.

Such an exorbitant demand also puts a strain on an executive's resources. An executive might put a job seeker in touch with one or two colleagues, but she will not, however, burden them by referring dozens of people. Executives must ration the kind of job leads and additional sources of information they can reasonably provide, just as they ration their own time.

Given these factors, if you want to make the most of an executive's time and resources, it's imperative that you establish as strong a connection as possible. In today's workplace, that means networking in a completely different manner, finding the new opportunities and exploiting them to achieve the most significant results.

NETWORKING IS NOT A TRADITIONAL BUSINESS RELATIONSHIP

Consider this: You're sitting around the dinner table and someone asks you to pass the jar of pickles. You pick it up, try to open it, and can't get it to budge. Your daughter taps the top of the jar with her fork a few times, but can't open it, either. Finally, your husband tries hitting it with the flat edge of his knife—but before he can try to open it, your son grabs the jar and opens it with little effort.

So who was responsible for opening the jar... your son? Well, he was the final link in the chain. More likely, though, it was the collective efforts of everyone along the way that contributed to that result.

When you think about it, networking works the same way. It often seems like a lot of work, and you may spend years getting to know people, and offering to do favors for people, without seeing very much in return. But, in the employment context, one small conversation, one interaction, even one minute can change everything—someone may resign or retire, or the company may acquire the budget to expand its headcount. All of a sudden, your efforts will have paid off.

When someone tells me that they found a new job through a network connection, they often talk about how frustrating it was that they "had to speak with ten people over an extended period of time" before they got hired. The implication, of course, is that the other nine connections were meaningless, or provided little or no value—and that isn't the case at all. Like the family with the pickle jar, it was the cumulative results of their previous networking that put them in that position.

Now don't get me wrong—I understand their frustration. After all, most business transactions are based on results. Either both parties receive an immediate benefit, or are at least aware of the benefit they'll receive in the future. If I sell you a car for $1,000, you get a car and I get $1,000. If you sign a contract with a personal trainer for six sessions, the trainer receives her fee and you'll learn how to perform an effective workout and, presumably, improve your physique.

But here's the situation: Networking is not a typical business relationship. You don't always know which effort will open the pickle jar, so to speak, or when that will happen. But, at the same time, there is an expectation of some mutual benefit, especially in today's workplace.

Networking was once a "take/take." You'd ask Sally to do you a favor, without offering her anything in return. Back when people had the time, energy, and resources to engage in a free flow of benefits and favors to others, this approach actually worked. Unfortunately, in the loyalty-free workplace this is no longer the case. Now, because of the cultural shift (and its effect on time and resources), people have become more selective about who they speak with and what information they share. So if you want Sally to provide you with job leads today, you have to give her something in return—and if she's like most people in the loyalty-free workplace, she'll likely require a benefit in exchange for her help.

> "The richest people in the world look for and build networks. Everyone else looks for work."
>
> **ROBERT KIYOSAKI**
> AUTHOR OF RICH DAD POOR DAD

So how do you navigate this? With so many people competing for Sally's attention, how do you stand out from the crowd?

Very simple: You reach out to her and offer *her* a benefit, without asking or expecting anything else in return. That way, Sally will remember you, so that when she does come across information that you can use, she might be more willing to share it with you.

NO ONE EVER STOPS NETWORKING

OK, that sounds easy enough. But if you're like most job seekers (particularly those who are in the early stages of their working lives), you might be nervous, embarrassed, or even ashamed to reach out to new people, or those you do not know very well. Well, first of all, you can be fairly certain that you have nothing to be embarrassed about. That's because *everybody* networks. Even those who are at the top of their game continue to network, because they know that networking helped them reach their success (and is likely at least partially responsible for keeping them there).

> Entrepreneur Janet Li, 51, sits down for a pedicure at the spa at the five-star Missouri hotel where she is attending an Asian-American leadership conference for women. To her surprise, she sees a well-known television personality (and highly sought-after speaker) in the chair next to her. The commentator asks Janet, "Why are there so many beautiful Asian-Americans in this hotel?" After explaining that they are there for a leadership conference, Janet invites the TV personality to speak at their conference the following morning. As soon as Janet mentions this, she is approached by the woman's manager, who says that her client will be leaving for Texas later that day. After presenting Janet with her business card and a folder with materials, the manager invites Janet to reach out to her directly to arrange for her client's participation on a future panel.

As it happens, Janet was just starting her business. So, imagine her surprise when she realized that the highly sought-after speaker was just as interested in networking as she was.

Remember, no one ever stops networking. The more you realize this, the easier it will become. Before you know it, you'll find that just about everything we do in life can become a networking opportunity, even a trip to the spa.

BE BOLD... BUT IN A WAY THAT WORKS FOR YOU

Early in my career, when I was learning how to negotiate contracts, a colleague said that if I wanted to let opposing counsel know that I was serious about a particular issue, I should bang on the table and storm out of the room. Being quiet and low key, I didn't think that tactic would work for me, but one time I decided to try it. When a lawyer from the other side made an incredibly offensive remark, I pounded my fist on the table, told him that I found his comments unacceptable, and stormed toward the door.

The only problem was that, in this particular situation, I was the head of a twenty-person bargaining committee. My colleagues, all of whom were seated around me, were completely taken aback—they'd never seen me react that way to anything before. And so, by the time I found myself in the hallway, I noticed my entire team was still seated at the table, unsure if they were supposed to have followed me out or watch me leave.

The point is, as you continue to network, no matter what industry you're in, you'll come across people who network aggressively, and those who use more passive techniques. You should know which style works best for you, and then modify it to fit your personality.

> Ralph Lorenzo, 46, is a pilot applying for a position with a major airline. As part of the interview process, Ralph meets with in-house recruiter Gail Pregman, 55. During the interview, Gail and Ralph discuss one of his former positions, which included flying a plane used to transport organs for a major hospital. Because Gail's son-in-law happens to be applying for a high-level administrative position at the same hospital, she finds this conversation particularly interesting. At the conclusion of the interview, Gail informs Ralph that she will conduct a reference check as the final stage of the process. One of the references she plans to contact is Dr. Seligman, a transplant doctor at the hospital for which Ralph once flew.
>
> After speaking with Dr. Seligman about Ralph's qualifications for the position, Gail asks Dr. Seligman if he might be willing to provide her with the name of a contact at the hospital where her son-in-law hopes to work. The doctor agrees. When Ralph is offered the pilot position at the airline, he calls Dr. Seligman to thank him. That's when he learned that Gail had asked the doctor for a favor on behalf of her son-in-law.

While Ralph was shocked that Gail had used his job interview as a vehicle to help a member of her family, Dr. Seligman was more forgiving. He simply recognized that Gail was an aggressive recruiter who saw every interaction as a possible networking opportunity.

Whether Gail's conduct was appropriate is open to debate. The point here, like that of the example with Janet and the spa, is that we will find ourselves in a wide range of situations that may present us with a networking opportunity. When the opportunity presents itself, we need to be ready to act if we hope to receive a benefit.

Now, what if you're the type of person who finds any conversation that's even remotely job-related to be beyond their comfort level? One way to overcome this fear is to remember that most people, to some degree, incorporate networking into their job search strategy. And since everyone has looked for a job at some point in their lives (and most of us will be looking for a number of different jobs throughout our working lives), when you do reach out to someone, chances are that person will have once been in the same position as you.

Another way to gauge your level of comfort is to imagine your reaction if the roles were reversed. If you were Dr. Seligman, and think you'd be offended by Gail's asking you a favor, then don't utilize that tactic. But if you see her request as a creative approach to networking, then consider using a similarly aggressive technique that's tailored to your personality.

HOW TO NETWORK PASSIVELY

As you can see, the loyalty-free workplace requires an approach to networking that is much broader than ever before. Once you grasp this, you'll find yourself networking without even realizing it.

Griffin Sampleton, 50, viewed his layoff from his business development job as an opportunity to transition to a new role leading a non-profit organization. While attending the funeral of the father of a former colleague, Griffin engages in small talk with one of the attendees and mentions that, while he is currently unemployed, he is aggressively pursuing a position with a newly established charitable organization honoring Reed Sanders, a young man who was senselessly murdered. It turns out that not only was the attendee involved in the organization, but he went to high school with Reed. At the conclusion of this brief conversation, the attendee offers to call the organization the following day to support Griffin's candidacy.

No, I am *not* suggesting that you should hand out your resume at a funeral. But if you're waiting in line to enter the church (or standing by the buffet table at the reception after the service), and you find yourself talking to someone about your work or family or children, that may become an opportunity to network passively.

Remember, networking conversations in the loyalty-free workplace are much different that the ones you might have had before. In most cases, you're neither asking for a job, nor even discussing your job. Instead you're merely gathering information to see if there might be a way to help the person with whom you are speaking, sometime down the road.

Jill Geller, 25, is a big fan of a Hollywood actress who was going to perform *Romeo and Juliet* in a nearby city park. As the area has limited seating, Jill and her friends line up on the sidewalk at 6:00am that morning in hopes of securing seats for the 8:30pm show. Of course, by the time Jill and her friends arrive, there are thirty other people waiting ahead of them, even at 6:00am. By the time Jill and her friends are seated (in the third row) at 7:30pm, there is a large group of people who had friended each other on Facebook and vowed to meet up for drinks at a future date, which they do. Five years after seeing that play, four members of the group who met that day are still good friends.

When Jill woke up that morning to get in line for the show, I am sure that networking was the last thing on her mind, especially since she and her friends were all employed at the time. However, by developing those friendships, Jill established a relationship with four people whom she might not otherwise have had the opportunity to meet.

You really never know when you will meet people that will become part of your network. More often than not, these relationships develop naturally, especially when circumstances require you to be in the same place with each other for a given period of time.

> "More business decisions occur over lunch and dinner than at any other time, yet no MBA courses are given on the subject."
> **PETER DRUCKER**

Mommy blogger Jennifer Davis, 46, is traveling with her husband and son in a first-class cabin to her cousin's wedding on the West Coast. Unbeknownst to Jennifer, her son is continuously kicking the seat in front of him. About a half hour into the flight, the woman whose seat is being kicked turns around and introduces herself to the son, adding that the kicking of her seat "seems to be in sync with one of the latest hits from the boy band One Direction." While Jennifer's son smiles, Jennifer apologizes for the disturbance—only to learn that the woman is a talent booker for one of the country's largest providers of content for satellite radio. As it happens, the talent booker is familiar with Jennifer's blog, and they vow to keep in touch. Eighteen months after that encounter, Jennifer self-publishes her first book. She reaches out to the talent booker and secures two radio interviews to publicize the book's release.

Anytime you attend an event where the attendees have something in common, it's an opportunity to forge a relationship. If you sit next to someone at a hockey game and learn that you have other common interests, why not suggest becoming Facebook friends or connecting via LinkedIn? It's not that different than exchanging business cards—in fact, assuming you have your smartphone with you, technology has made it possible to make the connection on the spot.

Angie Sills, 44, agrees to escort her friend to a charity dinner when her friend's husband is stuck at work. At the dinner, Angie meets the president of the board of the charity; the president mentions that the organization is having trouble recruiting new board members, which is critical to the future of the charity. Since Angie has been appointed to a different non-profit board through a placement agency, she offers to send the board president the information about that recruitment option. That information results in the charity finding three additional board members. When the president emails Angie to thank her for the referral, she takes note of the fact that the president was the head of sales for a large retail store. A few months later, when Angie's daughter is looking for a retail job to earn some income during her holiday break, she writes a short note to the board president and attaches her daughter's resume. The board president is more than happy to forward the resume to the recruiter assigned to hiring seasonal staff.

Just as you should have an open mind about using non-work situations to build relationships that might assist you professionally, the same holds true when it comes to the people with whom you currently work. While it is generally unwise to openly discuss your career plans with your direct supervisor, there is nothing to prevent you from selectively reaching out to your peers and the people who work in other parts of the company.

Administrative assistant Camilla Barker, 31, has some basic knowledge about graphic design. On one occasion, when her boss is unexpectedly called out of the office, Camilla provides copy editor Alexandra Devoe, 52, with help on the cover of her freelance project. Eight months later, Camilla shows up at the holiday party (which everyone at the company must attend). Never particularly skilled at small talk, Camilla is pleasantly surprised to see Alexandra by the food table and starts to ask her how the cover design turned out. In response, Alexandra informs Camilla that while the cover turned out well, she also realized she has no interest in the design side of the business and would much rather stick to copy editing. She goes on to tell Camilla that the business was expanding rapidly and was constantly looking for freelancers to produce covers. As it happens, Camilla would like to further develop her graphic design skills. When she mentions this to Alexandra, Alexandra puts her in touch with the company looking for freelance graphic designers. Camilla is eventually able to secure a significant amount of freelance work.

While you are working in a particular job, you should build whatever relationships you can, since those relationships may help you in your current situation as well as in the future. Not only that, when you leave a position, be sure to make a significant effort to stay in touch with your former colleagues. That way, if they are ever

> "Networking is an essential part of building wealth."
> ARMSTRONG WILLIAMS

in a position to hire you for a new role, or hear about an opportunity that might match your qualifications, they'll know how to reach you.

Remember, people want to work with people with whom they have a relationship. If you have a strong working relationship with a supervisor or colleague, odds are that you'll both want to re-establish that working relationship, if the situation presents itself. Why? Because you both know that such a relationship has worked before, and will therefore work again.

> Chief Sales Officer (CSO) Timothy Wagner, 46, works in a large insurance company and is recruited for a similar position at a large mortgage company. Timothy knows his success in his new position will depend on the strength of his sales team, so he conditions any potential offer on his being allowed to bring his own sales team (which he decides will be comprised of one person he is currently supervising, as well as two other dynamic salespeople he has worked with in the past). After some difficult negotiations, Timothy accepts the new position at the new company and is able to hire the three-person sales team he initially proposed.

Even if your prior supervisors are never in a position to hire you directly, this component of your network is important. Prospective employers place the highest value on referrals from people who have had personal and direct dealings with the applicants.

> Chris Hull, 28, applies for a competitive managerial position at a national chain restaurant in New York City. Chris reaches out to his prior supervisor, Jerome Danners, 39, and asks him to call the vice-president of operations (who happened to be Jerome's roommate in college) to vouch for his work. Jerome explains to the vice-president that Chris's managerial skills transformed a restaurant that had been on the brink of closing into one of the city's most popular restaurants. A few weeks later, Chris is offered and accepts the position.

In this case, Jerome is the ideal person to vouch for Chris because he has a direct connection with not only Chris (the person he was recommending), but the vice-president of operations (who had an influence in the hiring decision). However, even if Jerome didn't have a direct connection with the prospective new employer, this type of recommendation is still valuable to Chris because of Jerome's personal knowledge of his work.

Personal recommendations from people with whom you have worked directly are always given considerable weight in the hiring process. If you're Jerome, you're not likely to recommend candidates who are poor performers or problem employees, because that would reflect badly on you. Along the same lines, people are usually eager to recommend stellar candidates for positions that others are trying to fill. By doing so they are doing someone in their network a "favor," which increases the likelihood of the recipient doing *them* a favor in the future, should the need arise.

NETWORKING AT WORK IS NOT LIMITED TO WORK COLLEAGUES

As long as we're looking at networking from different perspectives, remember that your customers and your vendors can also be invaluable sources of leads and information.

> Television news anchor Dylan Landers, 36, is required to attend at least three charity events a year in order to promote the television station that employs her. At one such event, a resigning media relations associate is honored for her contribution to an organization. At the end of the evening, Dylan approaches the organization's executive director, with whom she had developed a strong working relationship. Dylan convinces the director that her long-standing relationships with the press would provide her with the ability to thrive in the newly vacated role.

Of course, Dylan took a risk by informing the executive director that she was seeking work opportunities outside of television news. But, in this case, Dylan had to reveal that—otherwise the executive director probably would not have considered her as a candidate for the vacancy. This brings us to our next important point:

IF YOU WANT PEOPLE TO CONSIDER YOU FOR NEW OPPORTUNITIES, YOU HAVE TO LET THEM KNOW

Dylan's story is a good example of how chance encounters in your current work situation can lead to networking opportunities. So how do you expand your network to include other people?

> "First, you have to be visible in the community. You have to get out there and connect with people. It's not called net-sitting or net-eating. It's called net-working. You have to work at it."
>
> **DR. IVAN MISNER**

I once attended a panel discussion for aspiring script writers. Near the end of the discussion, one of the attendees asked the moderator, an established script writer, how to 100-percent guarantee that no one in Hollywood would steal his script, which he was certain would eventually become the next blockbuster. The moderator asked if the script had been written and printed out. The answer was yes to both.

"Perfect," said the moderator. "When you get home, erase any digital copies, place the printed copy carefully under your bedroom mattress, and keep it there forever. This is your 100-percent guarantee the idea will not be stolen by anyone in Hollywood. Unfortunately, this is also the only 100-percent guarantee that your script will never be made into a movie."

OK, perhaps the moderator was being overly dramatic, but you get the point. If you want someone to buy your script, you have to let them know it's available.

How does this translate to your job search? Well, that's pretty simple: If you're interested in an opportunity that is outside your field of work, and would like to be considered, follow Dylan's example. Talk to the person who makes the hiring decision and tell them that you're interested. This is particularly important if you're out of work, or know that your current employment will end on X date in X number of weeks.

People who are already employed often hesitate to let others know they are looking for a job, for fear that their boss might find out. Or, if they've been laid off or terminated, they're too embarrassed or depressed to talk about it with others. Unfortunately, unless you open up to others at some point, the odds of finding the job you want are about as good as Steven Spielberg discovering your screenplay when you've hidden it under your mattress. After all, that's the entire point of networking. Unless you reach out to people, whether you're employed or not, you won't be in a position to receive any leads if and when they materialize.

> Amanda Lasher, 22, graduated from a liberal arts college in Boston. Unable to find a job, she moved back to the small Midwestern town where she was raised. Desperate for work, Amanda started to baby-sit for some of the families in her hometown. When most of the parents asked her about her future plans, Amanda became even more depressed. But in the case of one mother (Jenny Woods, 31), when Amanda said that she missed Boston and wanted to move back to a large city, Jenny offered to put Amanda in touch with her sister, who lived and worked in New York City. Amanda graciously accepted the offer and spoke to Jenny's sister, who put her in touch with a number of her friends who worked in temporary placement agencies in New York and New Jersey. Amanda was eventually placed in a temporary role in New Jersey, which led to a permanent role from which she could easily commute to from her New York apartment.

Instead of obsessing over her situation to the point of depression, Amanda should have realized that she was not alone. Indeed, in light of the current economy, many talented people have been laid off or are out of work, so the stigma of unemployment is not as great as it was before. And because people are changing jobs more often, once she started networking she was likely to talk to people who were in her situation not too long before.

Remember, modern networking is as much about building relationships as it is about finding job leads. Not only that, most of us have all kinds of potential networking opportunities right within our reach—and they don't always come from our peers or coworkers. *Anyone* who enters our life on a daily basis has the potential to help us, if we get to know them. In Amanda's case, let's say that, in addition to watching their kids, some parents have Amanda drive their children to school or after-school activities. That would put her in daily contact with those children's school teachers, activity leaders, soccer

> "A lot of fellows nowadays have a B.A., M.D., or Ph.D. Unfortunately, they don't have a J.O.B."
>
> **FATS DOMINO**

or Little League coaches, camp counselors (if she is baby-sitting during the summer), and so on. By reaching out and connecting with these people, Amanda makes them a part of her network, and she becomes part of theirs.

USE "SOFT TARGETS" TO EXPAND YOUR NETWORK

Now, what if you're currently unemployed, and you understand the importance of networking, but you have somehow convinced yourself that you're just not good at it? Perhaps you need to broaden your understanding of what networking entails. One way to do that is to start small by practicing on a few soft targets based on your personality. These are places where you naturally meet people, and those people might be great contacts, even though you are not necessarily seeing them for networking purposes. For example, when you see your hairstylist, your main concern is having your hair cut or styled. If you're like most people, you probably pass the time talking to your hairstylist. Why not let her know that you're looking for a new opportunity? If she's like most hairstylists, her regular clients will include people from all walks of life. She just might know someone who could help you.

Make a list of all of the people you know and feel comfortable with, regardless of where they work or if they're even working at all, and start talking to them. This includes friends, neighbors, people you do business with, prior supervisors, and past teachers. If any of these people have hiring authority, put them at the top of the list. After all, the end goal of networking is to interact with people who have the authority to offer you employment. Any time you have a direct line to a hiring manager, that gives you a jump on other candidates who don't have that kind of connection.

Then make a list of the activities you enjoy doing in your free time, be that softball, bowling, or working out at the gym. Next time you engage in those activities, reach out to new people so that you can expand your network. If you don't have great people skills, place yourself in situations where the discussion topics will be about something you are familiar with. If you're in a softball league, perhaps the team goes out for pizza and beer after the game. There, you can interact with others naturally without feeling coerced.

If you are not sure of where to start, many online networking groups can provide you with a great foundation. Meetup.com, for example, is a far-reaching global networking group that enables you to interact and build relationships with others with common interests, be they vegans, ballroom dancers, ukulele players, or people who read about philosophy or neuroscience. You can attend meetings to interact merely on a social level, or join groups that have more of a professional spin. For the most part, the groups and meetings are informal, so you can attend and participate in events on a frequent or infrequent basis. In addition, if you have a very specific interest, finding or even creating a Meetup group can help you assess whether there are others who work in areas you want to transition into professionally, as well as learn

> "It takes as much energy to wish as it does to plan."
>
> ELEANOR ROOSEVELT

about the types of professional opportunities that may exist in any given field. Plus, when you join Meetup, you'll have the opportunity to build a profile, which will be searchable on the Internet. In that way, your interests can lead to other opportunities.

School reunions are also great opportunities to expand your network quickly. Reunions enable you to reconnect with people that you once knew, and possibly rebuild those relationships. And since these days many school reunions involve graduating classes from more than one year, you will likely meet new people. These connections, regardless of how tenuous, have the potential to be very valuable.

Suppose you receive an email from a stranger who asks whether you might be willing to forward their resume and cover letter to the hiring manager at your job for a vacant position for which they applied. This person reminds you that they spoke to you briefly last summer at the Rutgers reunion. Because all graduates from an institution share a connection, you might be willing to provide assistance simply on that basis.

Another "soft target" is your local community. You could volunteer in your church or synagogue, or at a neighborhood charitable organization. In each instance, you'll meet people with whom you'll have a common bond, by virtue of the church or charity. Each person you meet is a potential connection who may help you down the road.

BE PART OF A CONFERENCE

While you're making that list, jot down some of your professional activities. With a little bit of research you can find some events, receptions or conferences where you can talk to people about their interests—and which will eventually lead to yours.

Now I realize that a lot of people suggest attending conferences to broaden their network, but I'm talking about something different. After all, there are a lot more benefits to a conference than just going to all the presentations. You can actively *become* a part of the conference yourself.

For one, if you have expertise in a particular topic, and you are comfortable speaking in front of people, volunteer to be a presenter. Even if you're not entirely comfortable with this idea, keep in mind that once you give your presentation, the audience will come to you. That eliminates the need for you to decide who to approach, and how. In addition, the process of delivering a presentation will give you invaluable insight into how you should build other relationships. Since you'll likely be approached by different people in different ways before, after, and perhaps during your presentation, you'll know what types of networking techniques will be most effective, and which fall flat.

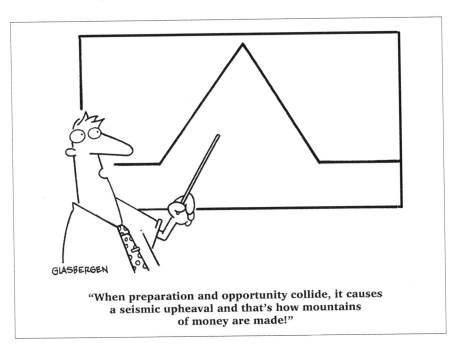

"When preparation and opportunity collide, it causes a seismic upheaval and that's how mountains of money are made!"

If you'd rather shun the spotlight, and you feel your strengths are more organizational in nature, you could volunteer to help organize the conference (which would include arranging for speakers). This will give you a prime opportunity to reach out to the people that you want to meet, and you'll do so with a specific purpose (i.e., securing their participation in the conference), which should alleviate any qualms you have about approaching them. Plus, when you attend the conference, you'll have a reason to meet the panelist face to face and thank them for their participation. This will give you a second opportunity to develop your relationship.

Another way to participate in the conference is to assist with registration. This, again, gives you direct access to everyone that attends the conference, but in a non-threatening way. And, if the conference allows it, you might be able to obtain a list of the attendees, as a way to follow up with the people you meet. Even if you can't obtain an attendee list, by participating in a conference on any level, you'll be interacting with the most active members of the sponsoring organization. Those are the people who usually have the largest networks at their disposal.

Now, what if you're concerned that, whether you give a presentation at a conference or become part of the conference committee, your boss might view this as an attempt for you to find another position? That's simple enough: Let your boss know about your participation and invite him to attend. For one, it will showcase your expertise, while allaying his suspicions. And because you'll be using your participation as a way of creating a long-term benefit, the presence of your boss should in no way impact the benefit you'll receive. At the event, you can decide on an ad hoc basis whether the timing is appropriate to mention your current employment situation to a panelist or attendee—or, as an alternative, you can focus on making the initial connection and delay the conversation to a time when your boss is not in the vicinity, and you will be more comfortable having a frank discussion.

YOU CAN'T SOAR WITH THE EAGLES IF YOU'RE HANGING OUT WITH TURKEYS

OK, now that you've identified people that you currently know in your personal and professional life, and you are placing yourself in situations where you will likely meet new people, how do you go about adding them to your network? Who do you approach first, and how can you do this in such a way that it becomes a strong connection?

> "The fastest way to change yourself is to hang out with people who are already the way you want to be."
>
> **REID HOFFMAN**
> AUTHOR, THE START-UP OF YOU

One way to start off is to remember the "broken window theory," which suggests that people act according to their surroundings. So, if you live in a neighborhood where everything is pristine, you tend to behave more professionally. But if you live in an area that is not maintained (i.e., broken windows, graffiti, and other signs of wear and tear), you might let some things slide.

How does this relate to the employment context? We tend to be drawn to those who have similar traits to our own. So if you associate and socialize with people who are positive, successful, and who also happen to earn substantial sums of money, then you will likely engage in behavior, both consciously and subconsciously, that will produce those same results. To this end, when deciding who to target first as you begin to build your network, look for people who support your goals and whose values reflect your own. The person may not be a friend, per se, but should represent the type of person you already are or would like to be. Conversely, if you find yourself surrounded by negative people who feel and act as if they are stuck in dead-end jobs with little hope for making improvements, you might want to distance yourself from them before their attitude hinders your own success.

Along the same lines, besides looking for those who will support you in this process, you want to align yourself with people whose earnings are either comparable to yours, or at the level that you hope to achieve.

Studies have shown that people tend to earn within 20 percent of the earnings of those in their social circle. Assuming this is true, this means we are motivated, either consciously or subconsciously, to stay within that range. So if you earn $125,000 per year, and the rest of the people in your network earn more than that, that might spur you on to find a position that increases your income. Today it's vital to reach out to those whose ranks you want to enter, and not limit your interactions to those who are already your peers. In some cases you may find that volunteering at a charitable dinner for museum patrons may be more productive than hosting a potluck dinner for your colleagues.

TURN YOURSELF INTO A TICK

Remember, in the loyalty-free workplace, no one ever stops networking. This is a long-term lifestyle change that will enable you to earn a growing and perpetual paycheck for decades to come. So, as you start to look for your first job, you also have to plan for the future.

If you've ever attended an independent film festival, you will notice that many films are cast with the friends, neighbors, and family members of the directors and producers—many of whom agreed to do the film for little or no compensation, as a favor to those involved in the project. Dispersed among those personal relationships, you will also see a number of other actors looking for on-screen exposure, not to mention the opportunity to meet all the people involved in the project (financiers, publicists, sound technicians, editors) as a way to expand their networks.

At one such festival, when asked by an audience member how to find a mentor and break into the business, one producer stressed the importance of seeking out new and young directors and screenwriters. Not only that, she encouraged the audience member to become "like a tick" and latch onto them *now*, before they experienced their first theatrical success. Otherwise, it would be too late—by the time these newbies achieve their theatrical success, you'd be competing with the hundreds of others who want to develop the same connection.

Therefore, besides reaching out to people with more experience than you (such as a hiring manager or executive), you should also reach out to those who have less experience than you. Jim in the mailroom may not have much influence now—but five or ten years from now, when you're prepared to leave your job and he's running his own company in the same field as yours, that's a different story. Not only that, by connecting with Jim now on the basis of future benefits, that shows him that you're committed to a long-term mutually beneficial relationship. Plus, being at a lower or junior level, Jim isn't as likely to be flooded with requests as his boss in the executive office. That lessens the competition for Jim's attention, and even his resources.

SAME AREA OF EXPERTISE

Of course, connecting with people who might help you in the future is just one component of your network. You also have to build relationships with people who can help you with your current search. You can start by looking for people who work in the same industry, and whose level of experience is similar to yours.

Here again, industry conferences and events can help you form connections. If you attend a conference related to your area of expertise, you'll likely learn about current industry-specific news and trends, which can help you as you plan for upcoming interviews. The people you speak with will likely know which companies are doing well and are likely to expand their staff, and which companies are having financial difficulty and may be downsizing or merging. If a merger is imminent, this could mean additional jobs if the business is changing, or layoffs in the event of duplicative service.

In addition, people in the same industry, and who have the same expertise as you, will likely know certain people in the industry who have vacated their positions for various reasons. As you speak with them and develop a rapport, they may be willing to share some personal information that may be valuable to you, such as whether they're about to be promoted, change directions in their own careers, or perhaps even retire. In sharing this information, they're letting you know that there may be a job vacancy in the near future, which you can monitor.

Of course, as we mentioned before, the real benefits of a conference go beyond attending. While you may run into some people that you already know, you will just as likely meet a lot more people that you don't already know. If you meet twenty new people over the course of the conference, that's twenty opportunities to expand your existing network. That, again, is one of the purposes of networking.

Is there a downside to networking within your own area of expertise? Yes, and it speaks to the nature of the loyalty-free workplace. Traditionally if you practice family law, for example, you'd probably build a network that included as many family law attorneys as possible, because the more attorneys you knew, the more likely it would be that someone in your network would know about appropriate jobs and share that information. In the old days, when most people stayed at their job for twenty or more years, this strategy made sense, because only a small percentage of working attorneys were looking for new employment at any given time.

In the loyalty-free workplace, however, people leave jobs more often. Today, if you go to a conference and meet twenty family law attorneys, most of them are looking for their next opportunity, just as you are. And because more and more people are competing for fewer and fewer opportunities, these twenty attorneys may be less inclined to share information with you, because they may see you as competition for a job they'd like to have.

Given the changing dynamics, should you therefore ignore people with similar areas of expertise? Not in the least! As we've seen, targeting people who support your efforts and share similar goals is a great way to start networking—but, remember, it's just the foundation. You will also want to expand your network by approaching people *outside* of your industry.

This idea may have seemed counterintuitive before, but in the loyalty-free workplace, it's critical. Why? Because by simply changing your surroundings you can significantly increase the value of your expertise and the likelihood that you will learn of opportunities for advancement.

SAME INDUSTRY, DIFFERENT AREA OF EXPERTISE

Consider this example: If you're a chef, and you're talking to other chefs about how to cook the perfect steak, depending on your cooking methods or level of expertise you may not stand out from the others. But, if you're in a room full of twenty-five-year-old novice chefs who are hosting their first dinner party, and you relay that same information, they're going to treat you like a rock star because you know something they don't.

Or how about this: If you're an insurance attorney, and you attend an event geared towards insurance attorneys, you're like the chef in a roomful of chefs: your colleagues will see you as a peer. However, if you as an insurance attorney go to a convention for insurance sales representatives, you'll certainly obtain many of the same benefits you'd receive at a conference for insurance attorneys (industry news, trends, forecasts, new opportunities for jobs, etc.). The difference, of course, is that because you come at the industry from a different angle (legal, as opposed to sales), the sales reps might see you as an expert. Just as important, they *won't* see you as competition for possible sales positions—and they *will* be open to sharing information about openings in their legal department. Not only will those sales representatives not be your direct competition, but also an insurance salesperson looking for a job may actually be eager to share information about a legal position with an attorney because (1) sharing the information has no detrimental impact on their job search; (2) the information is not valuable to them; and (3) more importantly, they could see sharing that information with you as a way to develop a connection with someone who may be able to provide a future benefit.

> "It isn't just what you know, and it isn't just who you know. It's actually who you know, who knows you, and what you do for a living."
>
> **BOB BURG**

In the loyalty-free workplace, you need to not only increase the size of your existing networking circle, but create new circles. That means expanding your network by networking in the right rooms. This will increase your chances of getting the best information, build your confidence, and really display your expertise.

Financial planner Branden Halpern, 46, left his lucrative job with an investment management company to start his own financial planning business. A ferocious networker, Branden attends financial industry conferences, meetings, and events frequented by Wall Street executives to secure clients and build his business.

Six months later, after securing only a few clients, he decides to attend some conferences for entrepreneurs, where he hopes to learn about some other ways to generate clients for his new business. There, Branden meets entrepreneurs from a wide range of industries: world-class hotels, prestigious academic institutions, large pharmaceutical companies, and major department stores.

Soon, Branden discovers that many of these entrepreneurs recently left their mid-level positions to launch their own businesses. Knowing that some of these entrepreneurs accumulated money in their 401(k) retirement plans, and that they probably had to move these funds from their former employer's plans into their own investment accounts, Branden recognized these entrepreneurs as a potential new client base. He was able to use these types of clients as a launching pad for his now-thriving financial planning practice.

When Branden attended conferences with other Wall Street executives, he certainly increased his network. But, once he started going to events for new or young entrepreneurs his efforts really paid off, because the entrepreneurs recognized the value of partnering with a financial planner like him. Not only did his expertise make him stand out, but he also expanded his network to a number of different industries to which he might not otherwise have access.

VALUE IS IN THE EYE OF THE BEHOLDER

When you start reaching out to other industries, make sure you're speaking to the right audience.

I once attended a sport memorabilia estate sale with a group of friends who had eBay businesses through which they earned income selling items. The young entrepreneurs looked for heavily discounted items (usually a 90 percent discount) that they could purchase and then sell online (at 50 percent off the list price). From their point of view, that's a win-win: They make a profit off their original investment, while also providing an item that a buyer might not otherwise find.

While my friends were clamoring for a particular hockey jersey and signed pair of sneakers, I stumbled on a box of women's clothes. Inside that box was a nearly-new pair of Gucci shoes, which I not only purchased at 90 percent off the department store price, but also still have as part of my wardrobe.

What does this have to do with networking? For one, as we saw from the example with Branden, people and things derive their value from those who are there to see them. To a roomful of sports memorabilia collectors, a pair of Gucci loafers has little, if any, value. But had those same shoes been on display in a second-hand clothing store, they would have gone for a lot more than what I paid for them. In addition, this situation illustrates the benefit of expanding your reach beyond one industry. After all, you never know where the next opportunity will surface. Though I cannot prove this, I would venture to say that had my friends purchased the pair of shoes I now have in my closet, they would have made more money from reselling those shoes than they did from the sales of any of the sports items they secured at the estate sale. In other words, you have to open your mind to all possibilities, even if they are nothing like what you originally contemplated. You need to remember the end goal of earning a growing and perpetual paycheck, so you can have the freedom to do whatever is truly important to you.

At the same time, when reaching out to a connection in the hope of procuring a favor, make sure they see the value of what you're asking in the same way that you do.

> Because she has significant experience creating work-life balance programs, Brenda Flukes, 53, was eager to apply for the vice-president position in the work-life department of a large computer manufacturing company. Brenda explains that she is reaching out to a number of people at the company to discuss the vacancy. Her primary goal is to arrange for an informational meeting with the CFO, who is the brother-in-law of an old college friend.

Given that Brenda has a personal connection with the CFO, I applauded her for "reaching for the top" to ensure that her resume is appropriately reviewed. At the same time, I suggested that approaching someone who held a different role at the company might yield a better result.

A CFO is concerned about the company's bottom line. While Brenda sees the potential value in investing in a work-life program (healthier employees mean a decrease in sick day use, which, in turn, could result in a significant increase in productivity levels), the CFO would likely see the costs involved (installing a gym in the office, offering additional healthy options in the lunchroom, and hiring a part-time nurse to staff a healthcare clinic) as expensive additions to the budget that he has to balance. An employee at a lower level might be more receptive to her ideas and, therefore, be more likely to help her get an interview (and possibly a job offer).

BE THE SMARTEST PERSON IN THE ROOM WITH YOUR EXPERTISE

I once taught a class in human resources management as part of a prestigious program at an Ivy League institution. Prior to the course I received a list of the executives who were taking the class, along with a lengthy document spelling out their accomplishments. The roster included surgeons, pediatric oncologists, doctors with credentials in multiple specialties, executives who were transforming the healthcare system, and people who were committed to reforming healthcare in impoverished areas. I remember how nervous I was heading into the class: Look at all these impressive accomplishments! Who was I compared to them?

On the first day of class, in the hope of calming my nerves, I asked everyone to introduce themselves and talk about what they hoped to achieve in class. As each explained their background, it became soon apparent that, for all their accomplishments, they had no idea what to do if an employee was rude to a patient, made an error, or called in sick on five summer Fridays in a row.

That's when I realized that in the context of that classroom, for that purpose, at that moment, *I* was the expert. They might spend the rest of their life curing cancer and helping other people, but on that day they were there in that classroom because they needed something from me.

This goes back to what we said about Branden and the entrepreneurs. If you want to land a job in the loyalty-free workplace, it's not enough to be the smartest person in the room. You need to be the smartest person in the room *with your type of expertise.* So if you're in a room where your skills are not valued (or perhaps they *are* valued, but someone else has more to offer), the simplest way to resolve the situation is to showcase your skills in a different room.

PAY ATTENTION TO PREREQUISITES

Now that you know which people to target for your network, and the best places to find them, how do you develop these relationships so that they become meaningful connections?

Anyone who has taken even a basic psychology course will tell you that people tend to feel more comfortable around people who are similar to themselves, and people want to help people who they think someday will be in a position to return the favor. Regardless of whether this is a conscious choice or not, this is the reality and should inform the way in which you network.

If you love animals, you've probably heard of the theory that as dog owners age, they start looking more and more like their pets. The premise, in short, is a variation of the idea that we're attracted to things that are familiar to us. It's not so much that people begin to resemble their dogs physically, but rather, that we select pets that look like ourselves because this sense of familiarity and comfort breeds positive feelings. While some of you may think that's absurd, not only is there a psychological explanation for this phenomenon, it once made the pages of *The New York Times.*

The relevance here goes back to the broken window theory. Just as we tend to start networking with people whose values and goals reflect ours, hiring managers tend to favor (and, in many cases, eventually hire) people who are similar to themselves. It's worth remembering this because some prospective employers will require applicants to have a particular qualification, on the basis of commonality. In some cases this occurs even if that qualification has no bearing on the individual's ability to perform the responsibilities of the job. It might even result in the disqualification of otherwise qualified applicants.

Though Kyle Chappen, 26, attended a Boston law school, she was fairly certain she wanted to return to New York to establish her career. Since her law school's career network was not well established in New York, her law school entered into a reciprocity agreement with a New York school to share job postings. According to the agreement, one person from the Boston school could visit the career center of the New York school and review their resources and internal postings, and then one person from the New York school could visit the Boston school and access their resources.

Because the agreement required a one-for-one exchange, it took a number of months for Kyle to finally receive notification that she could visit the New York career center. Taking full advantage of this reciprocity agreement, Kyle applied for more than a dozen positions for which she was qualified. Problem was, within a matter of weeks she received rejections from each of the prospective employers, indicating they did not even review her application because they were specifically looking for a graduate from the particular New York school where the position was posted.

In this case, prospective employers were more concerned with the prerequisite (having attended a particular school) than in Kyle's qualifications. Although the situation worked against Kyle (she could not take advantage of the vacant job postings in that school's career center), she did learn that alumni from this particular New York school were extremely loyal to one another and therefore inclined to help other alumni. That information could be useful to Kyle. Should someone who attended that New York school approach her for advice in the future, she could share her experiences and direct that person to the alumni postings for an immediate and valuable benefit.

In some situations, the desire for this common bond is even more fundamental. For example, some companies expect all new employees to pay their dues by starting in the mailroom and working up in the company ranks. Even experienced employees have to go through this sort of vetting to ensure that everyone at the higher level has had the same basic foundation. So, if you want to work for a company that adheres to this stringent process, then it would make sense to apply for a position at an appropriate rung on the ladder. In other cases, there may be a career progression that

> "Birds of a feather will gather together."
>
> **ROBERT BURTON**

occurs outside of a particular company, but within the industry in general. For example, a law firm may want its associates to have completed a year-long clerkship before they join the firm. Even if an applicant has developed comparable experience without ever having been a clerk, the partners may resist bringing in someone who deviated from the path.

The moral of the story, of course, is that if you apply for a job with certain requirements (such as a college degree from a particular college, or an advanced degree from any school, like an M.A. or Ph.D.), unless you clearly meet those requirements you should look for other opportunities.

ANY CONNECTION IS BETTER THAN NO CONNECTION

Some people in your network will become strong and direct connections, working in the same industry, and with whom you'll have a long-term and personal relationship. Some connections will be more tenuous, because they work in different industries, live in different geographic locations, or haven't interacted with you much. The point is, there's a strong correlation between the strength of the connection you have with someone and the extent to which they will be willing to help you. Knowing this— and understanding that people are inclined to help those who are like themselves—as you continue to draw connections from different sources, it's important to strengthen those connections as much as possible. This does *not* mean that you should underestimate the power of your tenuous connections, because they can also be extremely valuable. However, you should take advantage of any opportunities to strengthen your connections because this will result in an enhanced benefit.

When I was growing up, my family owned their own business. The running joke was that my parents liked to attach my resume to the invoices of their customers, as if to say that anything they could do to help me land a job could result in a generous discount. As a kid, I hated that. I was always afraid that someone would agree to place me in a job for which I was not qualified (and from which I would likely get fired), just so they could take advantage of the discount. Of course, this never happened. However, what I now know, and what my parents likely knew years ago, is that when applying for a job, any connection is better than none at all.

When a hiring manager posts a job vacancy, she might receive a hundred applications and resumes. Of those applicants, fifty may come from job seekers who are not qualified for the position, while another twenty-five may not be interested in the position, but applied anyway just to see if anything materialized. Still another five applicants may have some of the skills required for the position, but not all of them. That leaves a total of twenty applicants who might be suitable candidates. But, because she has limited time and resources, the hiring manager is not likely to call in all twenty candidates to delve further into their qualifications.

Again, I speak from experience. Whenever I was charged with reviewing resumes to determine which applicants should be invited in for an interview, I would often hope that someone, *anyone*, would call me with a name of an applicant whose resume I should look out for. At the very least, that gave me a basis to prioritize which resumes should merit further attention.

Remember, you're not the only one working in a loyalty-free workplace—so is the hiring manager. Assuming she's a skilled networker, the hiring manager is also looking to build connections and expand her network. Even if the requester has only a passing knowledge of that particular applicant, it requires little effort for the hiring manager to pull an applicant's resume from the stack, so she has little to lose by granting the favor. More to the point, by establishing a connection with someone who might be able to help her in the future, the hiring manager now has something to gain.

In addition, from the job applicant's perspective, finding a connection to a vacant position can set you apart in other significant ways. First, by asking someone to reach out to a hiring manager on your behalf, that shows the hiring manager that you're willing to go the extra mile to ensure that your application is reviewed. In today's environment, where "spraying and praying" is prevalent, this is particularly welcome.

ON THE OTHER HAND... DON'T SPRAY AND PRAY

What do I mean by "spraying and praying"? That's what happens when job seekers send out email blasts with their cover letter and resume in response to any and every position that even remotely matches their qualifications. While you never want to stop networking, you want to put some thought into the process so that it yields results. There's no point in sending out a query when you know you're not qualified for the position. That wastes your time, and that of the hiring manager.

"Never mistake activity for achievement."

JOHN WOODEN

HALL OF FAME BASKETBALL PLAYER
AND LEGENDARY COACH

Even if you do manage to hit pay dirt using the "spray and pray" method, use common sense and be respectful of the time and resources of others. When someone makes time in their schedule to meet with you, the last thing they want to hear is that you have twenty-two other people you need to meet that week. Along the same lines, when someone puts you in contact with a few of their colleagues for further advice, don't be imprudent enough to say that you were "already referred to them and have meetings scheduled."

It's one thing to network aggressively. But you don't want to appear overly aggressive, to the point where it makes you seem desperate, or even puts your current position at risk.

> Alex Jeffries, 64, owns a large hardware store. He would like to create a general manager position to assist him with the day-to-day management of his business. Alex has a long-time assistant manager, Kevin Ewing, 42, whom he has considered promoting for a number of months, but he is not convinced that Kevin is ready for the general manager role. To get a better sense of the type of candidates who might be looking for the job, Alex posts an anonymous listing online. Within two weeks, Alex receives 111 applications to his anonymous posting—one of which comes from Kevin, indicating he "works for a local hardware store with no opportunity for growth."

The modern workplace requires everyone to keep their options open—both employees *and* employers. In this case there is nothing wrong with Kevin's actions, especially since he provided neutral facts in his letter. Had he bad-mouthed his current employer, such as drafting a cover letter suggesting that his current employer made promises that he did not keep, this could have placed his current employment at risk.

I am certainly not suggesting that you openly advertise your networking activities, particularly if you are concerned about a vindictive employer. However, as we saw in the example with Griffin at the funeral, there are ways to let others know that you're open to other opportunities, without being overt.

EVEN A LOOSE CONNECTION CAN LAND YOU AN INTERVIEW

No question, much of the networking that takes place in the loyalty-free workplace is a *quid pro quo*, meaning the giving of a benefit is contingent upon the receipt of a benefit in return. Even so, there are people out there who will do favors for others (regardless of how closely connected they are) without looking for anything in return.

> Insurance agent Ashley Knight, 48, speaks at a panel sponsored by her college alma mater. During her presentation, Ashley mentions how her experience working for the company Innovative Insurance prepared her for her current role. After the conference, aspiring insurance agent Paul Asher, 31, sent Ashley an email thanking her for an informative panel presentation and letting her know that, after hearing about the value she derived from her work at Innovative Insurance, he looked into vacancies at the company and applied for two positions. Paul also attached his resume and cover letter and asked if she would kindly forward his information to anyone she knew who still worked at Innovative Insurance. To his pleasant surprise, Ashley said yes. Paul was called in for an interview.

Here we see two factors at work: Paul's aggressive networking and Ashley's altruism. The basis of Paul's connection to Ashley was that he saw her speak at a conference, went to the same college, and wanted to work at Innovative. Paul had nothing to lose by reaching out to her, and he no doubt made an impression by personalizing the request and citing the value he received from her talk. Though Ashley had no firsthand knowledge of Paul's qualifications for the position, because college graduates from the same institution tend to help fellow alumni (as we've seen elsewhere in this chapter), she was still willing to forward his resume and application to her contacts at the company. (One imagines, however, that she informed her colleagues that she could not speak personally about Paul's work. In most cases, a disclaimer such as that is enough to overcome any potential fallout, in the event Paul proved to be a less than stellar candidate.)

At the same time, while Ashley was not necessarily looking for anything in return, by forwarding Paul's resume to her former colleagues at Innovative she strengthened a number of different relationships. For one, her introduction, though tenuous, did distinguish Paul from the other applicants and may have had an impact on the company's decision to interview him. In addition, by providing Paul's application to her colleagues, Ashley puts herself in a position to ask a favor from them in return, should she need assistance in the future. But it also establishes a relationship with Paul. Assuming Paul gets the job (or even if he doesn't), Ashley has placed herself in a great position to ask Paul for assistance in the future should the need arise.

All of this should serve as a reminder to never underestimate the power of a loose connection. In fact, many studies have shown that job seekers are more likely to secure opportunities from so-called weak connections (i.e., friends of friends) than from their first-tier connections. Why? Think about it. If you and your close friends work in the same industry, and interact with the same group of people, you're probably sharing the same information about certain job openings. But when you reach out to someone outside that circle (such as a friend of a friend), that exposes you to a new network, with new sources of information that your close friends may not know about.

Brenda Graham, 36, and Elizabeth Frankel, 36, have been close friends since kindergarten. Brenda always wanted to work in magazine publishing, but she could never get her foot in the door. When Elizabeth reconnects with one of her favorite English professors, Deidre Lakes, 55, at a recent college reunion, Elizabeth suggests that Brenda reach out to Professor Lakes for guidance. Professor Lakes provides Brenda with the names of some editors who were always looking for creative content for their magazines. As a result of those connections, Brenda was able to get her articles published in a number of national magazines.

Just as Paul had a weak connection to Ashley, Brenda had a weak connection to Professor Lakes, since their only bond was their relationship to Elizabeth. Even so, Brenda was able to parlay that tenuous connection into paid work, plus a slew of valuable contacts. That strengthens the bond between Brenda and Professor Lakes. But it also strengthens Professor Lakes' relationship with Elizabeth, because she helped her friend, while also expanding the professor's own network (which now includes Brenda).

Taking it a step further, just as you shouldn't underestimate the power of your own weak connections, never underestimate the weak connections of others. Because circumstances always change in the loyalty-free workplace, a loose connection between two people today can become a strong one tomorrow.

> Desperate for a new job, Vinnie Sarda, 31, eagerly accepted an offer to work for a national bookstore chain, fully aware that the job had a high turnover rate because the head of the department was a known tyrant. Sure enough, within the first few weeks of employment, Vinnie learned everything he'd heard about his boss was true. To avoid the inevitable, Vinnie used LinkedIn to identify and contact Leo Alda, 31, the person who immediately preceded him in the position (and who reportedly resigned because of the way he'd been treated by the head of the department). Leo never responded to Vinnie's request for information. Not only that, Leo reached out to his former colleagues to let them know about Vinnie's attempt to connect with him.

Gathering information can be very useful, particularly in the loyalty-free workplace. However, Vinnie's fatal error was underestimating the strength of Leo's connections with his former colleagues at the bookstore. While Leo may not have left the company on the best terms, he still had a number of relationships with the people who worked there, so he immediately contacted them to ask how they wanted him to respond. When they told him "not at all," he followed their precise instructions. Leo likely did not want to ruin the relationship he had built during his time at the company, and giving his former coworkers the information about Vinnie was a way he could strengthen his bond to them. Although Leo's ties to his former coworkers were weak, they were certainly stronger than his connection to Vinnie, his replacement, whom he had never met—and who, it seems, was already trouble in his job after only a few short weeks.

WHY STRONGER CONNECTIONS PRODUCE BETTER RESULTS

While any connection, no matter how tenuous, is better than none at all, common sense tells us that a strong connection is more likely to yield the best results. If your sister asks you for a favor, you are more likely to help her than you would a neighbor, a friend of your neighbor, or the neighbor of a friend of a neighbor. The reality today, as we've seen before, is that people have limited time and resources. The amount of effort they will spend helping you will depend on the strength of your connection. This is especially critical, given the competitive nature of the loyalty-free workplace.

Working people are smart—they know that extensively sharing information about job leads will inevitably decrease its value. An executive who shares information about a job that hasn't been advertised knows that this can provide a significant benefit to those with whom he shares it. The information will be more valuable if the executive discloses it to just two people with whom he has a strong personal connection, and less valuable if he shares it with a list of people that he met only within the past six weeks. There's nothing earth-shattering about that—it's basic supply and demand.

Not only that, when you ask someone to introduce you to some of their connections, odds are that other people in their network are asking the same thing. No one wants to overburden their own networks. So when you make that request, you want to be sure that your friend is connecting you with their strongest connections possible.

Remember in the modern world, everyone you meet is a potential member of your network. Within this group, you will obviously have a wide spectrum of relationships. If you work for the same boss for ten years, your connection with her is not the same as the one with the guy you met last week at a local awards dinner. While both are part of your network, your connection with your boss is likely much stronger.

The approach to networking in the loyalty-free workplace is two-fold. You want to adopt new techniques to ensure that you have a connection to any position you apply for (regardless of how tenuous), so you can stand apart from the other applicants in the crowd. But, because stronger connections are always better, you should also try to make your weak connections strong, and make your strong connections even stronger.

Now, how do you go about strengthening your connections so that you always get the most out of them? By remembering one thing: Networking is not just about you and your needs—it's also about the needs of the people from whom you're seeking assistance. Keep that in mind and you'll be in prime position for earning a growing and perpetual paycheck, as we'll see in the next chapter.

SECRET # 5

"HOW CAN I HELP YOU?"

You already know that to set yourself apart from this intense competition, you cannot limit your networking to people in your immediate job circle. You need to develop multiple circles and connect with people in all of them.

But that's just the beginning of the process. Once you expand your network, you need to strengthen those bonds by showing the people in your circles that you are ready, willing, and able to help them, even when you need nothing in return. That way, your connections will be more likely to help you when you do need a favor. The key is to network in a way that shows your connections that it's not about *your* needs, but *theirs*.

Wait a minute, I hear you say. When you reach out to someone in your network and ask them for a favor (whether it's a job lead or an interview with their friend Joe, the hiring manager), by definition you want them to do something for you. So how I can say that "networking is not about you"—isn't that a contradiction?

Yes, it is... but, remember, we're not just talking about networking. We are talking about networking effectively in the loyalty-free workplace.

The people in your network are just as smart as you are. No matter how cleverly you couch the request, they know what you're doing and they know what you need. But, like virtually everything else in life, our ability to obtain the results we want depends on how we go about it. We can ask for the same thing in three different ways and receive three different responses, all with varying degrees of success.

That being the case, the best way to get the most out of your connections is to approach networking as if you're doing *them* a favor, instead of the other way around. Above all, that means adapting your style to the person you are meeting, whenever possible. If you know someone likes to discuss work over cocktails, then schedule a time to meet up for a drink. If they like to discuss business over golf, meet them on the golf course or driving range. If they prefer having business discussions over the phone, schedule a call at a time that works for them.

> "The successful networkers I know, the ones receiving tons of referrals and feeling truly happy about themselves, continually put the other person's needs ahead of their own."
>
> **BOB BURG**

Remember, you're the one who needs the favor. Why not make it as easy on them as possible? If you can satisfy the needs of your connections first, they will be more likely to help you satisfy yours.

Jerome Banks, 61, heads up the sales force of a large mortgage company. Though he leaves the company to join a competitor, Jerome wishes to stay in touch with his former sales director, George Richards, 53. While George would rather speak to Jerome sporadically as the need arises, Jerome wants to formalize their continued relationship and suggests that their original team have quarterly dinner meetings. A few months later, when George also decides to leave the mortgage company to set up his own training company, he sees this quarterly meeting as the perfect opportunity to talk to Jerome about his new project. Before long, he signs Jerome as his first client.

Of course, there's a lot more to adapting yourself to others than just working around their schedule. Depending on their personality, you may need to make other adjustments. The best way to determine what you need to do is to pay attention to the different types of networking personalities.

"SNEEZERS" SPREAD CONTACTS, NOT GERMS

Long before smartphones and electronic devices, people kept their professional contacts filed alphabetically in a device known as a Rolodex. Whenever you made a new contact, or picked up a new client, you'd write down (or type up) their contact information on a card and insert it onto the round spool. The fanciest Rolodexes had covers to keep the contact cards in pristine condition. Back when informational meetings were indispensable, I could always tell how successful a meeting was by calculating how long it took for the person to reach for their Rolodex, *and* how many names and numbers they were willing to give me. That was how it worked. You'd meet someone about possible job leads, and if they didn't have any leads themselves, they'd put you in touch with a few people who might.

In the workplace, and even in social circles, people who are generous with their connections are known as "sneezers." Sneezers are, hands down, the best people to have in your network. Sneezers know *everyone*. They know their postman and pharmacist by their first names. They bake cookies for their crossing guard because they remember that she likes chocolate. They can strike up a conversation with someone at the grocery store over which cereal they have in their cart and, by the time they're checking out, they've exchanged business cards. Everything they do, everyone they meet, is a networking opportunity.

> **"The bigger your Rolodex, the bigger your business."**
> **ANONYMOUS**

Sneezers are valuable not only for their large networks, but for their willingness to share their networks with others. Because sneezers appreciate the benefit of the relationships they've built, they are happy to connect other people within their network, so that they can achieve the same benefit.

The generosity of sneezers is not to be underestimated. Lots of people have expansive networks, but not everyone is willing to generously share their resources, for reasons we've discussed.

Of course, because networking is a give and take, if you're lucky enough to develop a relationship with a sneezer, you should be ready, willing, and able to "sneeze back," so to speak. Then again, because sneezers have such mammoth networks, odds are you won't be flooded with a steady stream of requests for favors. But if you are, you should be as generous to them as they were to you. I have a few sneezers in my network who, over the years, have become close friends. If they reach out to me, I do my best to help them. Even if I don't have the precise information the sneezer needs, I reach out to others in my network to be sure that I deliver.

> "The currency of real networking is not greed but generosity."
>
> **KEITH FERRAZZI**

STRENGTHEN YOUR CONNECTIONS WITH T.O.Y.s

In a fundamental way, our professional relationships are no different than our personal ones. Some people, such as sneezers, tend to be outgoing in nature; others are quiet and reserved. Regardless of their personality type, or how they choose to network, all of our connections are important, even the ones that seem tenuous—and, just like certain personal relationships (such as our spouse or significant other), nurturing our connections and keeping them strong requires time and effort. The single most effective way to strengthen a professional relationship is to give your connection something when they least expect it.

Now before you start worrying about what this means to your bank account, the kind of gift I'm talking about won't cost you anything—but it can go a long way toward helping you. It's a little something that I like to call a T.O.Y. (which is short for *thinking of you*).

Think about it. We appreciate it when our spouse gives us a gift for our birthday, or when a friend sends a get well card when we've been home sick for a few days. But doesn't the gesture mean just a bit more when it comes when we least expect it? Suppose your boyfriend sends you flowers today "just because," or your friend drops off a freshly baked pie, because they thought you might enjoy it. These little acts not only build and solidify existing relationships, but make it more likely that we'll remember the gift-giver in the future—not only on pre-determined occasions, but also "just because."

The same holds true within the context of networking. When you send someone in your network a *thinking of you* at a time when you're not looking for a favor, chances are they'll remember your kindness down the road, when you actually *do* need their help. You can think of it as a "favor bank"—and while I am certainly not suggesting that you keep a ledger, in the loyalty-free workplace it's always better to have more favors owed to you than the other way around.

T.O.Y.s are a particularly good way to strengthen your bonds with your connections once removed—you know, the people you know because you're a friend of a friend. In some cases, the reason for sending a T.O.Y. may materialize naturally; with other connections, you might have to put on your thinking cap. Either way, bear in mind that the whole idea behind sending out T.O.Y.s is to provide value to the other person. In other words, you're not just reaching out to people for the sake of doing so. Rather, you're letting the other person know that you are interested in building a mutually beneficial relationship.

> "Those who ignore the party/conversation/network when they are content and decide to drop in when they need the network may not succeed. It's pretty easy to spot those that are just joining the network purely to take—not to give. Therefore, be part of the party/conversation/network before you need anything from anyone."
>
> **JEREMIAH OWYANG**
> WEB-STRATEGIST.COM

The basic idea behind a *thinking of you* is to reach out to someone who is a weak connection that you want to strengthen, or to a strong connection that you want to maintain, and provide them with an unsolicited benefit.

> College professor Ashley Engle, 46, dedicates the last day of each of her classes to talk about the job search process. She always reminds students of the importance of developing their networks, building relationships, and remaining connected to the people in their network throughout the year, not just when they need a favor. One year, Ashley emphasizes to her students that those connections must be meaningful to the person to whom you are staying connected, and not something that might be characterized as a nuisance or intrusive. To illustrate the point, she mentions that, for the past three years, she has received an email on the first Tuesday of each month from one particular student, asking "Hi Prof, What's up?"

Besides being inappropriate and not meaningful, the email from Ashley's former student is a good example of what *not* to do when sending a T.O.Y.

Remember, the point of staying connected is to bring something of value to the other person now, so that they can bring value to you later. The last thing you want to do is bombard people with notes every few weeks, to the point where they see you as a nuisance. Use this technique sparingly, and with some common sense. Make sure you have a specific reason for reaching out to your connections. If you're not sure whether the T.O.Y. is appropriate, ask yourself how you would feel if you were to receive it. If you were to welcome such a communication, by all means hit Send. If not, then hit Delete.

Above all, be professional. Sending a T.O.Y. is an element of networking, so act as if you're on a job interview (after all, the primary goal is to land a new position). You want to connect with the best people possible, so present yourself in the best light possible.

HOW TO MAKE THE MOST OF YOUR T.O.Y.s

Now, what are examples of appropriate reasons for sending someone a T.O.Y.? Well, if you met one of your connections at a conference for entrepreneurs about ways to gain a larger market share of certain products, one imagines they would welcome a business article about how to gain entry into certain retail chains. If you spoke to someone about your recent vacation to Italy, perhaps they'd be interested in an article about the top ten European destinations for seasoned travelers.

"You were my imaginary friend and we had some great times.
But I haven't heard from you since I was five years old
and now you show up and expect me to give you a job?"

You can also connect with people in your network based on information you obtained through other channels. If you connected with each other via LinkedIn, you can learn more about their professional background and particular interests. If they have a Twitter account, you can follow them there. Not only is that easy to do, it provides you with real-time personal information about their hobbies, likes, and passions. If they don't have a Twitter account, set up a Google alert with the person's name. When you think about it, that's even easier—instead of you having to research them, the research will be done for you. If your new connection wins an award or is quoted in an article, Google will notify you immediately of the achievement. That gives you a perfect excuse for sending them a quick T.O.Y., congratulating them.

Another meaningful way to strengthen a weak connection is to offer advice related to your area of expertise. Depending on what you do for a living, and the type of people in your network, it's likely that some of your connections would benefit from your skill set. If you're a website designer, and you meet someone who is looking to launch a new business, why not have lunch with them? You can give them insight on how websites are hosted, the going rate for the creation and maintenance of a website, and other information that they'd probably like to know. If you work in publishing and you meet someone who wants to publish a book, offer them your phone number and let them know that you're available to help them navigate the industry.

> "Networking is an enrichment program, not an entitlement program."
>
> SUSAN ROANE

Once you've provided them with the benefit of your expertise, it's only a matter of time before they'll ask you about your career, your ambitions, and how they can help you. And, even if that conversation doesn't emerge immediately, at the very least you've strengthened an existing relationship, making it more likely that this connection will reciprocate in the event you reach out to them.

If you feel reluctant about reaching out to a weak connection, remember two things: No one ever stops networking, and everyone wants to expand their network. The latter point is especially true in the loyalty-free workplace. Just as you should always plan for your next job as soon as you start your current one, so are other people in your network.

Now, if you reach to a weak connection that happens to be worried about their job status, they probably won't want to open up to you about their current struggles. They *may*, however, be passively looking for their next opportunity—in which case, anything you can do to help them in that regard will likely be welcomed. Even if they're not currently looking for a new job, since they operate in the same loyalty-free workplace as you, they probably won't turn down an opportunity to expand their network now, in anticipation for a future benefit.

Sometimes, however, you may send a T.O.Y. to a connection because you'd like to speak with them about something that you need or wish to pursue. That's OK, so long as the meeting or conversation also benefits the other person. Perhaps, as previously suggested, you can offer them advice related to their job or interests, or refer a candidate for a job vacancy that you know they're trying to fill. Along the same lines, if said person works in the service industry or happens to own a store, you could patronize the store and/or suggest that your friends or colleagues do the same. Or perhaps you've learned through social media that they're looking for a new dentist, or an after-school tutor who specializes in algebra. Either way, the person across the table will receive some value from the exchange, which will make them more inclined to help you with what you need or wish.

USING T.O.Y.s TO INCREASE THE VISIBILITY OF OTHERS

What if you want to solidify a weak connection, but don't believe that you can offer them anything of value? Then use the T.O.Y. to introduce them to someone else in your network that may be able to help. Perhaps you can suggest that the three of you meet for a drink or dinner. Not only does this show your weak connection that you have a genuine interest in establishing a mutually beneficial relationship, it will make your connection with the third person even stronger because you're helping them expand *their* network.

> "Successful people are always looking for opportunities to help others. Unsuccessful people are always asking, 'What's in it for me?'"
> **BRIAN TRACY**

If you have strong writing skills and happen to work for a company with its own monthly newsletter, you could volunteer to write an article about a topic that you know would particularly benefit or interest the connection(s) that you'd like to strengthen. Perhaps you'd like to interview them for the article, in which case you'd use this T.O.Y. as the reason for your meeting request. During that interview, you can ask questions relevant to the article, then use that as an opportunity to find out more about their careers. Of course, you wouldn't be asking the interviewee for a job, per se—but you could use the conversation to lay the groundwork for a future conversation, should it be appropriate.

Assuming the connection is like most people, she will likely be flattered that you requested to interview them. Knowing that, they're more likely to help you in the future, as opposed to someone who merely sends them a generic email asking for an informational meeting. Plus, having their name attached to a meaningful article can increase their exposure and marketability. That benefits them, of course, but it also benefits you.

Writing the article not only provides you with instant credibility, but it makes you an expert—and, depending on where the article is published, it has the potential to reach a broad audience. This is itself a useful networking technique, because other people may reach out to you after reading your article in an attempt to broaden their own networks. In the event the article reaches only a limited audience (i.e., those who work in your company or industry), you can still post it on your LinkedIn, Facebook, and other social media pages, thereby expanding your readership. And who knows, you might be able to negotiate a payment for your article. Not only will that enable you to supplement your income, you could use it as a stepping stone for other freelance articles that you might want to write in the future.

If writing articles is not for you, there are other ways to increase the visibility of a connection that you'd like to strengthen. If you're working on a conference, invite them to be on a panel. If you teach a class, perhaps they might be interested in speaking to your students.

Remember, the point of a T.O.Y. is to do something for someone else, unsolicited. That keeps you in the forefront of their minds, and makes it more likely that they'll think of you, should an appropriate opportunity materialize.

ANOTHER WAY TO STRENGTHEN YOUR CONNECTIONS: FOCUS ON THINGS YOU HAVE IN COMMON

Let's go back to our conference example. Suppose you're on the committee to select speakers and panel members. You identify a potential panelist, speak with them on the phone a few times prior to the event, and follow up via email. On the day of the conference, you introduce yourself to the panelist and thank her for her participation, plus you exchange business cards with three of the people who sat at your table during lunch. By the end of the day, you've established four new connections (the panelist, plus your lunch mates), but since they're all new it's safe to characterize these relationships as "weak" at best. You should immediately expend some effort to solidify and strengthen those connections so they become meaningful additions to your network. How do you go about developing them so that they become strong connections? By sending T.O.Y.s, of course.

Start by looking for things that you may have in common with your new connections. Review their LinkedIn profiles (or perhaps Google them and see if they're on Facebook, Twitter, Instagram, or Pinterest) to learn whether you have mutual friends or interests. If you do have friends in common, perhaps your paths may cross again in the future. If you don't have friends in common, assuming you have shared interests, you can use that information as the basis for a possible T.O.Y., using the examples I've mentioned. The point is, first you connect, and then you find meaningful ways to remain connected so that the connection benefits both of you.

> "You cannot receive what you don't give. Outflow determines inflow."
> **ECKHART TOLLE**

Remember, even though these are professional connections—and the basic idea behind networking is to put yourself in a position that benefits your career so that you can maintain a perpetual paycheck—this doesn't mean that every single interaction must be geared towards that result. A strengthener can still be a strengthener, even if it's only remotely business related.

A copy editor for an advertising agency, Claire Danners, 31, has clients that include a number of well-known cosmetic companies. Among the perks of her job is that she receives three tubes of their premium face wash each month. As this amount is well in excess of what one person uses each month, most of her colleagues tend to decline the free products. Claire, however, graciously accepts anything that is offered. Then, she brings her free products to her bi-monthly college alumni networking meetings, where other group members are thrilled to receive them.

To Claire, the extra bottles of face wash have no value to her. Yet, as you can see, she uses them more or less as a T.O.Y., to strengthen connections that might otherwise be tenuous. This is not to suggest that Claire will receive a job offer because she gave a bottle of face wash to one college alumnus, or baseball tickets to another. But it is the sort of gesture that can pay off for her, one way or another, in the future.

T.O.Y.s ARE NOT ONE SIZE FITS ALL

Because the key to effective networking is keeping the other person in mind, you must be willing to modify your technique to meet the needs of the people in your network. This goes back to what we said about adaptability. We have different types of relationships with different types of people, and people value different skills and opportunities. That being the case, you may send an article to one person in your network, while requesting to interview another person for an article you are writing. If one connection is thrilled to be part of your article, then look for other opportunities to include them. Along the same lines, if a connection would rather not be interviewed (or wants to talk, but doesn't want to be quoted), assure them that their comments will remain off the record.

Remember, everyone loves to receive T.O.Y.s, but there's more than one way to give one. There's no point in pressuring someone into accepting something when they don't see the benefit. Instead, consider using other T.O.Y.s to develop that connection.

HOW TO NETWORK BACKWARD

You know how some relationships just click from the start? That's how it is with networking. With some connections, you'll know right away whether they're willing to help you—you don't have to spend too much time worrying about the solidity of the relationship, because it strengthens itself on its own. For example, say your former supervisor asks you to help her daughter get a job interview. You make a few phone calls and, before you know it, one of your referrals ends up hiring her. You can bet that this particular supervisor will be more than willing to return the favor down the road. Similarly, if you're a chef and arrange for a former client to receive a significant discount for her son's graduation party dinner, this may be a good time to take advantage of that connection... particularly if you're not sure about the future stability of your current job.

> "If your ship doesn't come in, swim out to meet it!"
>
> **JONATHAN WINTERS**

If you have a particularly strong connection, then you should network backwards to use it most effectively. Instead of looking for people who have connections at the companies where you're seeking employment, look for vacancies at the companies where those strong connections will be in the best position to provide assistance.

After receiving a jury summons, transit authority executive Lea Ravitz, 53, spent four days in a packed waiting room. During that time she bonded with another woman, Susan McBride, 37. By the end of the fourth day, both Lea and Susan were excused from jury service; however, the two women exchanged business cards and vowed to keep in touch.

When Susan returned home, she reviewed the transit authority website and applied for positions that matched her qualifications. She also sent Lea the cover letters and resumes she submitted, and asked for her assistance. Lea was more than happy to pass the resumes on to the hiring recruiters for the positions. On the strength of Lea's recommendation, Susan's applications were immediately reviewed.

What if Susan found no positions at the transit authority that matched her qualifications? Should she have looked for a job elsewhere? Not necessarily. There might still be a way to make use of her new connection. While some companies post all of their jobs on their own website, there may be listings for other transit authority jobs that are posted in other places. One way to find out is to go to the company website, log on to the job site as a guest user, and scroll down the application to the drop-down box that asks where you learned of the particular opportunity shown on the screen. In that box, you'll likely see a number of options, ranging from certain job boards, conferences, or other places where the company recruits (such as indeed.com or LinkedIn). Jot down each of those options—in all likelihood, those are places where you might find additional job vacancies.

SEVEN WAYS TO MAKE THE MOST OF YOUR CONNECTIONS

Now let's suppose you've been delivering T.O.Y.s for quite some time and you're at the point where you'd like to take advantage of some of the benefits of those strengthened relationships. How do you achieve the best results?

1. MAKE A THOUGHTFUL AND STRATEGIC DECISION.

Remember, effective networking requires an effective strategy. So when you're ready to reach out to someone for assistance, come up with a plan: Learn about who you're going to target, and how you will maintain and strengthen those relationships. As you come to these decisions, put yourself in the other person's shoes—if you think you'd be offended if they were to ask you for the same favor, then don't ask. Or, if you think they wouldn't mind helping you, but would rather hear you ask in person instead of through an email, then by all means ask in person. The idea, of course, is to use the method that will yield the best result.

2. BE BOLD. BELIEVE IN YOUR PLAN AND EXECUTE IT WITH CONFIDENCE.

This may go without saying, but there's no point in carrying out a plan if you don't believe it will work. So once you develop your strategy, embrace it, and then execute it in a bold yet respectful manner.

> "Feeling confident—or pretending that you feel confident—is necessary to reach for opportunities. It's a cliché, but opportunities are rarely offered; they're seized."
>
> **SHERYL SANDBERG**

When I was in law school, the school would rent out a number of hotel rooms where interviews were held. We were given a list of room numbers where our interviews would take place, along with a reminder that students would be walking in and out of the interviews in tightly scheduled 20-minute increments. As you might imagine, due to the compressed schedule, some interviews ran late as the day progressed.

When it was time for my first interview, I approached the designated hotel room. Though the door was closed, the sign in the hall said clearly, "Knock on the door." Being somewhat nervous, and not wanting to interrupt the people in the room in case the interviewer needed more time, I tapped on the door very gently. No response. Ten minutes later, I knocked again—I wasn't sure that they'd heard me the first time, and besides, I certainly didn't want the interviewer to think that I was late for my scheduled appointment.

Well, it turns out the interviewer *did* hear the first knock. Next thing I knew, he swung open the door and told me rather curtly, "Yes, we know you're waiting, but as all of our appointments are running late we'll need a few minutes."

Later than afternoon, I had a second appointment. Once again, the door was closed; once again, I knocked very gently. That time I waited patiently for someone to come to the door. Fifteen minutes after my interview was supposed to start, the interviewer opened the door—only this time, she opened the door not because she was ready to see me, but because she hadn't heard my quiet knock and wanted to check with the reception desk to see why I hadn't arrived.

From this I learned, "Either enter big, or don't enter at all." The same holds true for networking.

When you reach your target connection on the telephone, carry yourself with confidence. Act in a manner to make the other person comfortable with your request and willing to agree to it. There's nothing worse than hearing a job seeker talk incessantly about how *"I know I'm asking for a big favor, and I would understand if you declined, but I really would appreciate it if you would kindly consider…"*

If you believe you're making a reasonable request, go ahead and ask. Your target connection will let you know whether they accept or decline. If he does say no, simply move on to the next target. Assuming you have a large network and a comprehensive plan, all you need to do is keep moving down the list until you receive an affirmative response.

3. BE SPECIFIC.

Once you have the person on the phone (or sitting across from you), be very specific as to what you want. Do not ask for a job (the person will likely know this is the eventual goal) and, ideally, explain what you have to offer in return. More often than not, people are willing to provide assistance, especially if they will receive a benefit in exchange.

Do not place the person in an awkward position that forces them to say no. Instead, provide them with some alternatives. If you're asking for an interview for an article you are writing, ask whether they would be comfortable having their comments in print, or if they might know of anyone else with similar expertise who might want to

> "The odds of hitting your target go up dramatically when you aim at it."
>
> **MAL PANCOAST**

have these discussions. If they're reluctant to provide an interview (or cannot because of company policy), ask if they will refer you to specific professional organizations or networking groups that might have members willing to participate.

4. MAKE THE FAVOR AS EASY FOR THEM TO GRANT AS POSSIBLE.

If you'd like Sally to provide you with a reference letter, don't leave it up to her to figure out what you need. Provide a description of what you hope the letter will accomplish and, depending on your prior history with Sally, consider giving her a summary of what you'd like her to highlight. You might even want to email her some bullet points that she can easily incorporate. If Sally is like most people, she's busy with her own work, so it may take a while before she writes the letter. By the time she gets around to it, the last thing you want to hear is that she doesn't have the address or the name of the company, or the title of your job and what exactly you did.

5. BE PROACTIVE. AVOID VAGUE PROMISES THAT MAY OR MAY NOT BE CARRIED THROUGH.

Never leave the meeting with an agreement that the other person will "contact you if an opportunity arises," or "get back to you if they come up with other ideas." You will never know if an opportunity never arose, or if they just plain forgot about your meeting. Instead, be proactive. Suggest that you follow up with them in two weeks to see if they came up with anything.

6. BE RESPECTFUL. TREAT ANY FAVORS THAT ANYONE OFFERS YOU AS IF THEY WERE A GIFT.

If you're like most kids, your mother always taught you to thank people whenever they send you a birthday gift—regardless of whether you already have the same item at home, or if it's the wrong size (or was intended for a four-year-old boy, and you're a six-year-old girl), or if it's something that you would never, *ever* use under any circumstances. As the saying goes, it's the thought that counts. When someone gives you something, you accept it graciously and show your appreciation.

This lesson holds true in networking, especially in the loyalty-free work-place. To achieve the best results from your networking efforts, you have to make it seem like it's not about you, but entirely about the person whose help you need.

7. REMEMBER THAT TIME IS MONEY.

This also goes without saying, but when reaching out to people in your network (regardless of the reason), remember that the time they spend helping you is time they could have spent doing something else. This is particularly true in the service industry, where people are paid for their time and advice. If your friend Alice owns a clothing store, you'd never ask her to let you have that brand new dress for free. But if Alice is a career coach with her own practice (and as such earns money by selling her time), if you call Alice and ask her for some impromptu job-search advice, you are essentially doing the same thing.

This isn't to say that Alice won't help you, or that you should never ask anyone to donate some of their time. The point is, when someone does take the time to help you, don't forget to thank them.

Along the same lines, when someone does you a favor (whether it's free advice or potential job leads), there may be times when they provide you with information that you already have. When that happens, be profes-sional and thank them anyway. Even if they don't follow through on what they promised to do—or provide you with something other than what you asked for—it is inappropriate to complain about it.

Dora Winters, 26, reaches out to her father's business associate William Perkins, 55, for potential job leads. After suggesting that Dora contact his brother, Jason, for some advice, William tells her to follow up with him after they speak, in case William has additional ideas for her to pursue. Dora schedules a call with Jason, but he cancels on her two times. When they do eventually speak, Jason seems unin-terested in speaking with Dora, and provides her with what she considers to be generic advice ("Just keep doing what you're doing and eventually things will work out"). After the conversation, Dora calls William and tells him that Jason rescheduled the call a few times and did not provide any meaningful information.

In this case, Dora was out of line bad-mouthing Jason and the advice he gave her. What she should have done was simply tell William that she spoke with Jason and "is still looking for new opportunities." Instead, by showing her ingratitude, Dora hurt herself in a number of ways. First, she insulted William's brother, which will likely impact her relationship with William. Assuming that he is close to Jason, William may no longer be inclined to help Dora to the extent he would have originally. In addition, should William share Dora's complaint with Jason, that could cost her the opportunity to add Jason to her network. After all, when you're looking for a job, you never know where your next opportunity will come from, so it never hurts to establish and maintain connections with as many people as possible. Even if Jason proved to be of no help himself, perhaps someone else in Jason's network could have given Dora a lead.

NEVER LET ANYONE REGRET THAT THEY DID YOU A FAVOR

While we're on the subject of gratitude and networking, here's a story that illustrates the old adage about not looking a gift horse in the mouth.

Once when I was on the way to my college dining hall, I saw a man holding a sign saying that he was homeless, had not eaten in days, and was desperate to feed his wife and two children. An hour later, as I exited the dining hall, I packed three peanut butter and jelly sandwiches, three apples, and three cookies into a lunch bag and delivered them to the man. When I handed him the bag, he asked what was inside. "Peanut butter and jelly sandwiches, apples, and cookies," I said. To my surprise, he said that he and his family would accept only a hot meal.

Granted, it's possible that the man or his children may have been allergic to peanut butter and jelly (or simply didn't like them). Still, I was taken aback by his comments. Not to sound harsh or unsympathetic, but if he was truly desperate (like his sign indicated), would he really reject anything but a hot meal?

There have times when some of my students have reminded me of the man with the peanut butter sandwiches. One of them will tell me that they're "desperately looking for a new job and need assistance right away." While I am always happy to offer them leads when I can, it amazes me how many of them respond by telling me, "Sorry, not interested in that position."

When someone in your network reaches out to you, even if it's for a position that isn't a perfect match, don't make them wish that they'd never helped you in the first place. Instead, be gracious about it and ask them to keep you in mind for other future opportunities.

Does this mean that you should pursue that particular lead? No, but if you frown on your connection now, he may doubt your motives and be less inclined to help you in the future.

Remember, effective networking comes down to strategy. Good strategy includes choosing your words wisely—both when you make the request, and when you respond. After all, if you tell your contact that you're "desperate," that suggests that you will consider anything and everything. When you come back and tell them you're "not interested," that will make them wonder just how desperate you are. Was the position that bad a fit, or were you not interested because it paid only $65,000 a year, and you want to make at least $80,000?

Plus, when you reject a job lead because you're not interested, you could miss out on other benefits that are not readily apparent. The position may not be quite what you're looking for now, but you never know where it might lead.

Justice Studies college professor Ken Hasten, 55, learns about an unpaid summer internship opportunity in a security firm. Knowing that his former student Shari Goden, a recent college graduate, is looking for a permanent position, he forwards the information to her. When Shari tells Ken that she isn't interested in the internship because she is only pursuing permanent paid opportunities, Ken emails the lead to the rest of his students. Some time later, Ken learns that the student who accepted the internship was subsequently offered a permanent position at the security firm.

Anytime someone personally reaches out to you with information about an opportunity, you should show your appreciation. This is particularly important when it's unsolicited.

Remember, when you send a connection a *thinking of you*, you're offering them something of value. You're telling them that you kept them in mind by sharing information that could help them. The same holds true when you *receive* a T.O.Y., especially from a former teacher.

College professors have many students, as do teachers of any continuing educational program that you might've taken. When a former instructor reaches out to you directly with a job lead, he's saying that he recognized something special in you. That's why he gave the lead to you, and not anyone else. For that reason, former teachers can be valuable members of your network and their influence should not be taken lightly.

In this case, besides missing out on an opportunity for a permanent job, Shari hurt herself in other ways. First of all, because she appeared ungrateful for his assistance, Ken may decide not to provide her with future leads. Further, even if Ken provided Shari only with information about permanent positions, that would have excluded her from considering temporary paid positions that might lead to a permanent paid job (which is often the case in today's workplace).

In addition, by rejecting the internship outright, Shari missed out on the chance to forward the lead to other people in her network. Just because the job wasn't suitable for her, it could have been an ideal T.O.Y. to send to someone else.

> Kim Ricketts, 51, runs into her former administrative assistant Sarah Jenkins, 31, at a hockey game. Because her current assistant is about to go out on maternity leave, Kim is looking for a temporary replacement and asks Sarah whether she is currently employed. Though Sarah has since earned an advanced degree and no longer does administrative work, she tells Kim she may know someone interested in the position. From the hockey game, Sarah emails a former neighbor who runs a mentoring program for recent college graduates. By the next morning, Sarah provides Kim with three potential candidates for the temporary role.

Instead of blowing Kim off (as Shari did with Ken) and saying that she wasn't interested, Sarah saw this as an opportunity to strengthen two connections. First, by providing Kim with three candidates for the vacancy, she "banks a favor" by providing her former boss with a T.O.Y., which might be valuable should she need a job reference. Plus, by forwarding the lead to her former neighbor, Sarah solidifies that connection, which may also result in a return benefit in the future.

NEVER REGIFT A PRESENT THAT ISN'T EXCLUSIVELY YOURS

That said, if you decide to forward a T.O.Y. (or "regift" it, as Jerry Seinfeld would say), make sure that you are only sharing information that is yours to share.

> College student Joelle Anderson, 20, asks communications executive Laurie Reynolds, 44, if they could have a 15-minute phone conversation to discuss Joelle's search for a job in the communications industry. Laurie says yes, based on

Joelle's email stating that she reached out to Laurie because Laurie graduated from the same communication program in which Joelle was currently enrolled, and because career services referred Joelle to her. During the conversation, Laurie provided Joelle with a number of job leads, the names of a few contacts, and information on two conferences that Joelle should attend to continue building her network. Laurie also provided Joelle with her personal email address and suggested that she keep in touch. Joelle thanked Laurie profusely for her time, adding that her advice was incredibly valuable.

Over the next two months, Laurie received six emails from other school alumni requesting informational meetings. All of the email senders stated that they received Laurie's personal contact information from Joelle.

Just because someone does a favor for you, that doesn't mean they'll do the same favor for someone else—especially when they don't know them. At the very least, Joelle should have asked Laurie first whether it was OK to share her contact information.

WHY SAYING THANK YOU AND UPDATING YOUR STATUS ARE GOOD STRATEGIC MOVES

We've talked about the importance of acknowledging people in your network whenever they help you. Not only does that cement your connection, but many successful companies expend significant resources because they recognize its benefits. For example, eBay tells its top sellers that "sending your buyers a thank you note after a purchase can be a great way to strengthen your seller-buyer bond. But besides that, it can also be a great way to increase your repeat sales." Toward that end, the website has even developed a "Thank You Emails" app in which sellers can notify individuals of other top-selling items on eBay, while also thanking them for their business. Knowing that people tend to buy items from people with whom they have established a connection, this not only makes sense, but is good business.

Besides thanking your connections whenever they help, be sure to update them as soon as possible should your status change. Not only does this strengthen your connection, this can help you avoid a potentially embarrassing or awkward situation that could wreck your relationship.

> After applying for a position with a local temporary agency, Maria Glanville, 33, asks her former supervisor, Sean McShane, 51, whether he knows anyone who currently works for the agency. Sean responds that he does not know anyone personally, but will reach out to others in his network to see if they have any connections—which he does, by sending out several emails and making a few phone calls. Two weeks later, after yielding no results from his efforts, Sean emails Maria, letting her know that he wished he could have been more helpful. In response, Maria thanks Sean and tells him not to worry: She already received a job offer last week, after reaching out to another connection.

We've talked before about how people today have limited time and resources. Knowing that she reached out to Sean—and knowing that Sean had taken the time to reach out to others on behalf of her—Maria should have let Sean know *right away* that she secured a new position and no longer needed his help. Instead she let a week go by, which wasted Sean's time. That's the sort of oversight that could hurt Maria in the future.

Remember, effective networking is about developing relationships, not destroying them.

> Marketing director Cate Singleton, 28, must put together a panel of experts to discuss how to leverage social media and other emerging technologies. After contacting a former college professor, Lenny Yaguld, 62, Cate and Lenny brainstorm ideas for potential speakers. Lenny gives Cate the

contact information for three people that he believes would add significantly to the panel, one of whom happens to be a retired colleague Albert Raver, 67. Four months later, after running into Lenny at a function, Albert jokes that he is going to start charging Lenny a fee each time he volunteers him to speak at a conference. Unbeknownst to Lenny, Albert had spoken on three different panels at the request of Cate, for no remuneration.

You should not make the same mistake as Cate, *period*. It is common courtesy to follow up with everyone you speak with as part of your networking process, to let them know how things materialized. This is particularly important if you receive a benefit.

Cate showed that she did not understand a fundamental rule of networking: When someone refers you to an opportunity, what you do is a reflection of the people who helped you. In this case, Cate's failure to acknowledge Lenny for his referral of Albert could also make Lenny look bad—for all we know, Albert may have felt that Lenny slighted *him* because Lenny didn't thank Albert for participating on Cate's panel. This is because people are judged by their referrals.

> "Silent gratitude isn't much use to anyone."
>
> **G.B. STERN**

Melanie Glover, 59, an executive vice-president at a large media company, recommended the son of a former client for a paid internship with her company. Melanie told the hiring committee that she had no prior interactions with the applicant, nor could she vouch for his work; nonetheless, the committee hired the son. As it happened, the son did not fare well in the program and was asked to resign. To this day, members of the hiring committee continue to hold Melanie responsible for the bad hire, while Melanie herself considers it a professional and personal embarrassment.

RESPECT THE NETWORK OF OTHERS

When someone provides you with a referral, you become an extension of that person's network and reputation. Because any misconduct will hurt not only your reputation but the person who recommended you, you should act in a professional and respectful manner at all times.

> Television producer Bruce Savante, 44, hires five interns each semester through the internship program at a local community college. At the conclusion of the program, most of the students (including Nikki George, 21), connect with Bruce on LinkedIn. After reviewing Bruce's 223 connections, Nikki sends multiple emails to the on-air talent who are in Bruce's network, telling them that she "is desperate to break into the industry and will do anything to make it happen."

This dovetails back to our example with Laurie and Joelle. Just because Nikki is connected to Bruce, that doesn't necessarily entitle her to ask others in his network for a favor—especially if the request is generic, one-sided, and provides nothing for them in return. Rather than approaching Bruce's network in this manner, Nikki should have asked Bruce first, perhaps by sending him a T.O.Y., so that at least *he'd* receive some benefit from granting the request. Then, within that context, Bruce could assess whether it's worth introducing Nikki to someone in his network. But because she didn't, that could hurt her connection to Bruce. In addition, anyone in Bruce's network who received Nikki's invite would probably assume that she contacted them with Bruce's consent. If they viewed her actions as intrusive, that reflects poorly on Bruce, which could damage his relationships with them.

Nikki should also avoid networking in this manner because it's an example of "spraying and praying." As we saw in the previous chapter, spraying and praying is a tactic whose success rate is dubious at best.

HOW TO NETWORK EFFECTIVELY WITHOUT BEING OBVIOUS

As you incorporate these new techniques into your life, before long you'll notice that the line between networking and ordinary conversations will start to blur. This will come in handy, in the event you're concerned about networking in a way that might upset your current employer. With that in mind, here are a few ways to network passively, but just as effectively.

First, in your current role you should always pay attention to who is being hired, who is resigning, and who is being promoted. Depending on your work circumstances, this type of information should be easily accessible, so you can stay on top of changes in personnel, regardless of whether you're looking to make a move. In addition, interacting with your colleagues is never a bad thing. For one, besides the fact that they will likely become an integral part of your network, if you're the type who feels more comfortable confiding in a very small group, you can ask them to keep an eye out for appropriate positions. Plus, as we've seen before, we often learn about people moving or resigning or needing additional staff, just by engaging in small talk.

Let's say Jane tells you that her spouse is interviewing for a new position. Depending on where he works and his area of expertise, that bit of news could mean a potential opportunity for you. Even if Jane's spouse is inter-viewing for an opportunity in another geographic location, that could still be useful to know—if Jane's husband is hired, he'll have to relocate, which likely means that Jane will be moving, too. Voila… that's a job vacancy in your own company, which only you know about.

Updating your LinkedIn profile on a regular basis is another great way to network passively. Just by virtue of being posted, your profile is accessible 24/7 to recruiters who might have suitable opportunities. Keep in mind, though, the key words here are "on a regular basis." If you haven't been on LinkedIn in a long time, then suddenly start following companies to see which ones are hiring, that tells the other people in your network (which likely includes current colleagues) that you're exploring other opportunities. But if you maintain a consistent online presence, by the time you are ready to make your move, no one will know the difference. In addition, those who maintain an active online presence will be in the best position to receive job leads at the right time (and in the event an opportunity comes at an inopportune time, you can simply decline).

Your passive job search can also include developing and maintaining relationships with recruiters. Most reputable recruiters value confidentiality and will help you search discreetly. You can also utilize the job boards that offer anonymous settings—but if you do, proceed with caution. After all, as you advance in your career and achieve targeted accomplishments, it would not be difficult for an employer to learn your identity through basic Internet research.

Keep in mind that just because you are networking passively, this does not mean you stop sending out T.O.Y.s. In fact, the best time to send out a T.O.Y. is at a time when you're merely keeping an eye open for other possibilities. The point is to consistently be looking for information and opportunities that will provide you with a benefit, as well as for information that will benefit others. This, in turn, will strengthen your relationships and ultimately benefit you.

LinkedIn is a great source of T.O.Y.s because it is a stream of current information about employment transitions. If someone in your network announces that they have accepted a new position, and you know that a former colleague would be a perfect fit for the vacated job, why not send a quick email to let her know about it? Along the same lines, if a recruiter contacts you to discuss a job that doesn't quite match your qualifications, why not recommend another candidate from your network who might be a better fit? You can offer both of these T.O.Y.s with minimal effort, plus there is a potential for both your former colleague and the recruiter to benefit from the

"You have to learn the rules of the game. And then you have to play better than anyone else."

ALBERT EINSTEIN

information you share. And, regardless of whether a benefit materializes, by sending these T.O.Y.s you have strengthened two relationships, increasing the likelihood that these two connections will provide you with assistance when you need it most.

Networking in the loyalty-free workplace is not always about looking for a job, or collecting business cards. Instead, it's about building relationships with the people behind those business cards and LinkedIn profiles. Just as you never stop looking for your next position even as you start your current one, you never really stop networking. Everything you do, every connection you make, is a potential key that can open the door to another opportunity.

Remember, it's a brand new day. The dynamics of the workplace may have changed, but there are more opportunities to find a job than ever before.

Think of your network as a VIP pass—another powerful tool that can help you navigate the loyalty-free workplace. And now that you know the lay of the land, with the help of these secrets *and* your VIP pass you are in a position where you can always identify job leads, secure employment offers, and maintain a perpetual paycheck, regardless of the circumstances.

ACKNOWLEDGMENTS

First, I want to thank my family: Marge and Aaron; Stacey, Jeff, Logan, and Davis; Jessica, Eric, Danica, and Jamie; and Melissa and Jariel. Each of you has always supported everything I set out to do and encouraged me to continue to pursue my goals, even when others suggested I pursue a different path. I know how fortunate I am, and I hope this book makes you proud.

This book may be about the realities of the loyalty-free workplace, but I'm incredibly lucky to have many amazing, talented, and loyal friends and colleagues. Marisol Abuin, you are a true friend. Thank for you for continuously reminding me that the process is the process, and I had to hunker down and forge ahead. Thank you also to the following individuals for their professional advice and friendships: Scott, Beth, Aidan, and Zoey Atkins; Judith Bass; Lou Bellardine; Dave Biderman; Jen Biderman ("B"); Charlane Brown; Dominique Bravo and Eric Sloan; Ann Burdick; Terri Caldes; Tom Carpenter; Irene Dorzback; Sheila Foster; Sheila Garvey; Hope Goldstein; Rosemary Griffin; Greg Hessinger; Joan Homkow; Alexis Hurley; Ken Husserl; Harvey Jacob; Jack Klinge; Marci, Jason, Harper, and Sloane Kroft; Sharon and Fred Kroft; Ryan Kroft and Adam Zeller; Dannielle Kyrillos; Ivy Lapides; Beth Wang Llewellyn; Mike McPherson; Becky Nelson; Debra Osofsky and Lenny Cassuto; Elena Paraskevas-Thadani; Lori Perkins; Marsha and Morey Rosenbloom; Susan Grody Ruben; Parisa Salehi and Burk Finley; Grace Trojanowski; Ana Venegas; Jayne Wallace; Tiffany Wysocki; and Ronnee Yashon.

A very special thank you to my amazing writing group, made up of not only best-selling authors but great friends: Erin Brady (www.erinbrady-author.com), Val Grubb (www.travelwithagingparents.com), and Sarah Price (www.sarahpriceauthor.com).

One of the many important lessons I learned throughout this process is the importance of selecting and relying on the best possible team. I could actually write a full-length book about the process I undertook to find the right team members, and the person best suited to know that this is definitely *not* an exaggeration is Ed Robertson. Ed, thank you for all of your work helping me to pry off my legal hat, streamline my writing, and create a user-friendly book that I know will be valuable to a wide audience. This final product would certainly not have been the same without your contribution. In addition, although it would be difficult to list everyone who so generously reviewed different parts of this book, I would be remiss in not acknowledging my amazing friends Jayne Bower, Adrienne Garafalo, Annette King, Linda Lupiani, and Mary Beth Wenger, who literally sharpened their pencils to perform a line-by-line review of the book as part of the final review.

And, as you might surmise, there is much more to writing a book than the writing itself. This became evident to me as I started to identify some incredibly talented professionals to help me with the presentation and marketing of it. Cartoonist Randy Glasbergen, I am thrilled that your cartoons are included in this book. Anna Kaiser, Mark Levine, Rachel Littera, Julie Lundy, and Christie Rears, thank you for your hard work and contribution. I look forward to working with each of you on future projects.

ABOUT THE AUTHOR

The extensive practical experience Lori B. Rassas has gained as an advocate for both employers and employees—in all phases of the employment relationship—has led her to develop a pragmatic approach to the navigation of career issues.

Lori B. Rassas, Esq., is an SPHR-certified employment attorney with close to two decades of experience. She received an LL.M in Labor and Employment Law from New York University Law School; a J.D. from the George Washington University Law School; and a B.A. from Tufts University. She has counseled employees in all phases of their careers, including individuals looking for their first jobs, individuals who have lost their jobs, and those who are changing careers. She has also advised employers on how to identify the best job candidates and build strong working relationships. Her first book, a textbook entitled *Employment Law: A Guide to Hiring, Managing, and Firing for Employers and Employees* (Wolters Kluwer, 2nd ed. 2013), lays out, in clear and concise terms, much of what she has learned about the legal rights and obligations of both employers and employees.

Lori currently has her own consulting practice offering training workshops, providing guidance on employment law and human resources matters, and working with individuals trying to navigate the workplace. She also regularly gives career advice to students from diverse populations through her work as a member of the adjunct faculty at The Mailman School of Public Health of Columbia University, Fordham University School of Law, The Scheinman Institute on Conflict Resolution at Cornell University, and Berkeley College. Lori is also a recognized expert on employment law and career issues, and has been quoted in a number of publications, including *The New York Times, CNNMoney, Fortune, USA Today College, Newsday, American Medical News,* and CareerBuilder.com.

Contact the author on LinkedIn, visit her website at www.lorirassas.com, follow her on Twitter (@lorirassas) or connect with her consulting practice on Facebook at www.facebook.com/loribrassas.

A FINAL FAREWELL

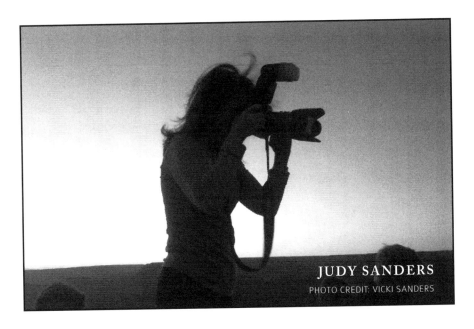

JUDY SANDERS
PHOTO CREDIT: VICKI SANDERS

"Life is like a camera, just focus on what's important and capture the good times, develop from the negatives and if things don't work out, just take another shot." **UNKNOWN**

Last, but certainly not least, I want to pay a special tribute to my long-time friend Judy Sanders, who lost her courageous battle with cancer. Judy was a treasured daughter, sister, aunt, friend, and long-time television newscaster who eventually became the official photographer for three

New York governors. Judy lived her life and tackled her work with an unwavering passion, even when faced with her devastating diagnosis.

For a number of weeks after Judy and I said our final goodbye, and Judy's medical team said she would no longer be with us, I cautiously answered my phone when her name appeared, expecting to hear her family member informing me she had passed away. Instead, I was met with the sound of Judy's distinct voice, giving me the name of "just one more person" who traveled to the Berkshires to say their own goodbye, and who Judy identified as one more person that I *really* needed to meet and could *definitely* help me to make this book a success. That was Judy, looking out for everyone else and planning for future successes, even until a few days before she passed away.

Judy, I will always treasure our friendship and remember how incredibly supportive you were of everything I was working on, and of my writing of this book in particular. You took charge of your life, along with your career, and soared to great heights using many of the strategies laid out on these pages. I hope that you would have been pleased with this final product, since you were definitely a part of it.

Made in the USA
Middletown, DE
08 July 2015